HAUNTED
BROMLEY

HAUNTED
BROMLEY

Neil Arnold

The History Press

This book is dedicated to Jez – rock on!

First published 2013

The History Press
The Mill, Brimscombe Port
Stroud, Gloucestershire, GL5 2QG
www.thehistorypress.co.uk

British Library Cataloguing in Publication Data.
A catalogue record for this book is available from the British Library.

ISBN 978 0 7524 9778 5

Typesetting and origination by The History Press
Printed in Great Britain

CONTENTS

Acknowledgements 6

Introduction 7

one   The Bromley Poltergeist & Others   12

two   Shivers at Shortlands   25

three   Haunting at Biggin Hill   27

four   Spooks around Beckenham   34

five   Orpington Oddities   43

six   Eerie Bickley   50

seven   Peculiar Penge   53

eight   West Wickham Weirdness   55

nine   St Mary Cray Strangeness   59

ten   Legends of Pratts Bottom   61

eleven   Horror at Hayes   63

twelve   Scary Sundridge   65

thirteen   Uncanny Chelsfield   66

fourteen   Chills at Chislehurst   74

fifteen   Encounter at Elmstead   88

sixteen   Mottingham Mystery   89

seventeen   Anomaly at Anerley   90

eighteen   The Petts Wood Ghost   92

nineteen   Ghouls of Green Street Green   94

Bibliography   95

ACKNOWLEDGEMENTS

Many thanks to the following people who have supported me not just in writing this book, but over the years. Firstly, all my love to my mum Paulene, my dad Ron, my sister Vicki, my wife Jemma and my grandparents, Ron and Win. Many thanks also to my publisher The History Press plus *News Shopper*, *Your County*, *The Victoria Advocate*, *Daily Telegraph*, Malcolm Hayes, Richard Thompson, Colin Goddcn, *Loaded*, David Spencer Smith, Paul Masters, British Newspaper Archive, Nick Redfern, Darren Naish, Jonathan McGowan, Medway Archives and Local Studies, Terry Hunt and Jason Desporte at Chislehurst Caves, *Daily Mail*, John Love, *The Robesonian*, *The Petts Wood & District Advertiser*, *Country Life*, *The Gentleman's Magazine*, *The Bromley Record*, *Kentish Times*, *Orpington Times*, *Beckenham & Penge Advertiser*, *Kent Messenger*, *This Is Kent*, *West Kent Mercury*, *Bromley Times*, *Bromley Post*, *Western Mail*, Marie-Louise Kerr at Bromley Museum, *Fact or Faked*, The Why Files. Special thanks to Suzanne North and staff at Bromley Archives and Local Studies, Chris and Janet Parsons and Emma Rodrigo for the illustrations.

All photographs taken by the author.

INTRODUCTION

If one flicks through the pages of any local ghost book, or attempts an internet search of ghosts in relation to Bromley, you'll find an alarming lack of stories. This is rather unusual considering just how much ground the Bromley borough covers – almost sixty square miles in fact. Maybe, due to the fact that Bromley sits on the Kent/London border, this means it has been ignored by a number of researchers when looking into its eerie history.

Bromley was first recorded as Bromleag in a charter from AD 862. The name is said to mean 'the place where broom grows.' It has also been known as Broom Leigh. The parish of Bromley was once recorded by author E.L.S. Horsburgh in 1929 as '…consisting of some four to five thousand acres of land…to the extent of one-fifth of it, nothing but woodland and waste even as late as the close of the century.'

Bromley as a market town is mentioned as being just ten miles from London. The outer London borough of Bromley is a sum of many parts – being one half urban, the other rural, taking in Chislehurst, Penge, West Wickham, Beckenham, Biggin Hill, Locksbottom, Petts Wood, Orpington, St Mary Cray, St Paul's Cray, Hayes, Eden Park, Elmers End, Chelsfield, Crofton, Derry Downs, Anerley, Sundridge, Goddington, Elmstead, Farnborough, Kevingtown, Leaves Green, Keston, Pratts Bottom, Plaistow, Park Langley, Bickley, Southborough, Bromley Green, Bromley Park, Green Street Green, Mottingham, Ruxley and part of Crystal Palace. A majority of these locations feature in this book.

Folklore surrounds a well in Bromley. It is known as St Blaze's Well (also known as St Blaise's) and was once said to have curative powers. Over time the well became less frequently used and was eventually filled in but discovered again in 1754. The chalybeate spring is said to have iron-rich waters. The word chalybeate derives from the Latin chalybs, meaning steel. Numerous curative wells are dotted about the British countryside, some long forgotten whilst others, such as the healing spring at The Pantiles in Tunbridge Wells, are celebrated. St Blaze's Well can be found at the old Bishop's Palace, also known as Bromley Palace which is a manor house once occupied by bishop's from the twelfth to the mid-nineteenth century. In 1973 Bromley Palace became a Grade II listed building and in the early 1980s became part of the Bromley Civic Centre.

The waters of the healing spring were tested in 1756 by a surgeon named Thomas Reynolds who concluded that the waters were much richer than those at Tunbridge Wells. The well can be found at the edge of a small lake, which it feeds in the grounds of the civic centre. Interestingly, the area of the well is said to be haunted by an unseen presence.

Bromley also has a hint of smuggling history, something one wouldn't normally expect considering that a majority of Kentish smuggling yarns originate from coastal and marshy areas such as Romney Marsh. In 1910 a chamber, some 18ft in diameter, with a depth of 8ft was uncovered at Chelsfield. The chamber was believed to have been prepared and used by smuggling gangs, possibly as a place to hide and also conceal their contraband.

The borough of Bromley includes some of Kent's most intriguing tourist attractions, including the caves of Chislehurst which stretch for around twenty miles. This eerie labyrinth worms its way some 3 metres below ground into a heart of darkness. According to the Chislehurst Caves website these tunnels 'were dug for chalk used in lime burning and brick-making for the building of London.' The public were first allowed access to the network of tunnels in the year 1900 and in the swingin' 1960s, and

not so swaggering '70s, they were used for concerts and parties. Hard to believe that just a few decades previous the passageways were used as an air-raid shelter during the Blitz and more than 15,000 people were housed there.

Bromley borough is home to a museum, which can be found at Church Hill in Orpington, and the area has also been known for a few famous residents, such as naturalist Charles Darwin and author Enid Blyton. Rock star David Bowie once resided in Bromley.

The borough also harbours Biggin Hill, known for its airport and considered one of Britain's most haunted locations. Considering how close it is to London, the borough of Bromley is also noted for its green parks and open spaces, and in the heart of the town sits The Glades shopping centre on the busy High Street.

In the autumn of 1976 Bromley was caught up in an Unidentified Flying Object scare. Several residents awoke to the news that a strange, metallic-looking disc-shaped craft had been discovered on a golf course in the town. News spread like wildfire and the police were soon on the case. A handful more of these 'saucers' were found elsewhere in the country. As things got out of hand the truth finally came out. It took a newspaper reporter to discover that the discs were manufactured by hoaxers. The jokers were a group of students from Farnborough who, never in their wildest dreams expected their prank to blow up the way it did. They had merely, for the measly sum of £30, constructed the saucers and filled them with melted bread dough – to resemble their version of alien goo! Their plan was simple, to raise money for charity as part of their college Rag Week. And so, armed with a pencil and a map they simply drew a line from Somerset to Kent and decided to plant six of their man-made discs at certain points. The hoax would take a fair bit of time as only one craft could fit into a vehicle. During the early hours of 4 September 1967 two small teams drove to the designated spots under the cover of darkness and placed their UFOs. Each disc measured 20 inches in depth and 30 inches in width.

This isn't the only sky-related anomaly to feature in Bromley lore. In fact the following story suggests that the borough is far stranger than anyone could have imagined. In 1797 a peculiar episode took place involving the then Bishop of Rochester, Samuel Horsley and his family at Bromley House. In a letter, later reprinted in *The Kentish Notebook* of 1892, he records:

Bromley House – July 10th, 1797 – 'Sir – The forenoon of this day (July 10th) was remarkably sultry, with little sunshine, except for about two hours and a half from noon. The greatest heat was about 3 o'clock when the sky was overcast again. At that time the Thermometer already in the shade, at a window on the north side of my house, and so fixed as to face the east, was at 81 degrees. But a little before it was taken to 77 degrees, and the Barometer at the same time, which in the morning had been at 30,08, was sunk at 30,03. Just about this time I observed the cows and Welsh poneys in my paddock all galloping towards the yard, as if something had frightened them. The sky was overcast with dark lowering clouds,

the swallows were flying very low, and from many appearances I apprehended that a heavy thunderstorm was approaching. We had sitten down to dinner (perhaps about 5 or 10 minutes past four) when a young Lady at table suddenly exclaimed in great surprise, that 'the hay was all falling about the garden.' Running to the window I saw many little handfuls of hay falling gently and almost perpendicularly through the air upon my lawn. Going to the front door, I saw the same sort of shower descending upon the grass on the contrary side of the house, and found my gardiner and labourous gazing at it. I observed a large black cloud coming over the house with a very slow motion from south to north, or nearly in that direction. Fixing my eyes steadily on the middle of that cloud, I saw several of these parcels of hay, one after another, dropping in appearance from the bosom of the cloud, and becoming first visible at a great height in the atmosphere. They descended with a very slow motion and with a very small deviation from the perpendicular in the direction in which the cloud moved. The atmosphere all this time was remarkably close and still. Not a leaf of the trees moved, not a breath of air was stirring, and my own hay was lying motionless in the field. Towards the evening a light breeze sprang up, which soon died away again; and the whole day has passed off without thunder, rain, or storm of any kind. The specimen of this hay, which I have the honour to send you, is the aggregate of two of the little parcels picked up by myself on opposite sides of the house.'

Centuries later odd things were still falling from the skies of Bromley. On the 28th October 1967 something very unusual fell from the sky and crashed onto the roof of a house in Bickley. A Mr John Boatwright was startled by the sudden crash on the roof at his home and so decided to investigate. He found an object measuring some 2ft in length that had taken out telephone wires on route to the roof. The sound of the object hitting the house was so loud that Mr Boatwright's neighbour heard it too. Bromley police were called out to investigate the strange fall and took the 2 inch round object away in a bucket.

In some instances of poltergeist phenomena, as mentioned in the case of the poltergeist in the Bromley segment, objects such as coins and stones have materialised from nowhere as if falling from the sky or the roof of a building. In this case the object was not believed to have fallen from a passing plane as there were none in the area at the time. No further details of the weird episode were forthcoming so maybe a mischievous spirit was to blame.

I write this book during a festive season. As the cold nights draw in, there is a layer of glistening frost on the ground. The leaves that remain on the stark trees are crisp and white and the only lights that puncture the darkness are those twinkling Christmas decorations in the distance. Christmas, for me anyway, isn't just a time for giving and receiving presents, but a time for telling stories, and there is nothing more powerful than that of the Christmas ghost story. Author Charles Dickens wrote what is without doubt the most famous festive ghost tale, *A Christmas Carol* but any good spook tale is suited to be told round a crackling log fire. I hope the stories I've chosen in relation to the borough of Bromley tingle your spine just as the winter weather does. I always tell people that it's not important whether you believe in ghosts, but it is important to have mystery and imagination in our lives. Of course, some stories contained herein are relatively vague; they exist as anecdotes passed down through generations, probably at Christmas, and also All Hallows Eve. Other stories however seem to have a sinister edge, and come from the mouths of those who actually experienced them first hand. These are the tales so hard to dismiss, so, before you scoff at *Haunted Bromley*, just remember, ghost stories, in whatever form, have existed for many, many years. Not every alleged encounter can be dismissed as hallucination, hoax or the result of the witness in question being in the company of too many spirits of the pub kind! Ghosts will always exist as lore, long after you and I have passed over, and I'd like to think that there's something beyond this earthly plateau. Maybe we'll never find out what lies beyond the veil and if, after all there is nothing, then so be it but the eye witness accounts suggest otherwise. However, for now, let's entertain ourselves with another set of creepy tales, best suited to a stormy night of raging gales and pattering rain. And, as I stare from the window of my study I wonder just what manifestations lurk out there in the darkest corners, not just of our woods and streets, but of our minds, because let's face it, it is the power of the mind that keeps these bone-chilling stories everlasting. And so, I offer to you my latest batch of tantalising tales, in the form of *Haunted Bromley*. Strike the match, light the candle and let us take a wander into the darkness …

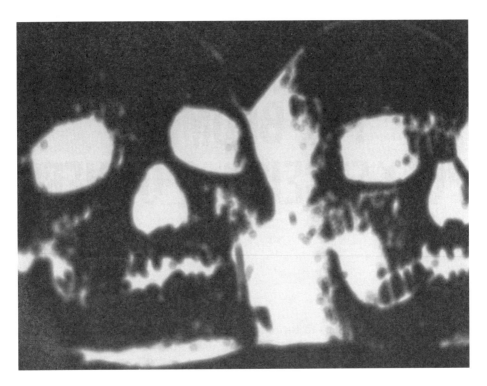

(Image created by the Author)

The Author

Neil Arnold is the author of many books including *Paranormal Kent, Haunted Maidstone, Haunted Chatham, Haunted Rochester, Shadows in the Sky: The Haunted Airways of Britain, Haunted Ashford, Shadows on the Sea: The Maritime Mysteries of Britain* and *Mystery Animals of the British Isles: Kent*. He has written for magazines such as *Fortean Times, Paranormal* and *Fate*, and runs ghost walks through the cobbled streets of Rochester (www.hauntedrochester.blogspot.com) and the dark woods of Blue Bell Hill (www.bluebellhillghostwalk.blogspot.com) near Maidstone.

'The mere mention of a ghost causes a bit of controversy. Men scoff and women shudder, and you are considered a halfwit if you believe in them...'
Peggy Martyn Clark, Secretary of Kentish Authors Group (1964)

1

THE BROMLEY POLTERGEIST & OTHERS

Author John Dunkin refers to Bromley as being 'pleasantly situated on a hill, on the high road from Hastings to London.' There is an obscure legend which claims that 'Bromley church' was originally built elsewhere at Widmore (situated one mile east of Bromley) but one dark night was plucked from the land by unknown forces and placed where it sits today! Science fiction writer H.G. Wells was also born at No. 46 Bromley High Street, in 1866.

Poltergeist!

In April 1973 a series of weird events plagued an allotment shed in Bromley. Over the course of fifteen months psychic investigators would be called to the allotment to delve into a mystery that would become known as the 'Bromley poltergeist'. The shed in question belonged to members of the Kentish Garden Guild, those being Mr Tony Elms and Mr Alf Taylor. It all began one afternoon when Mr Elms claimed that several powdered substances stored in the shed began to hit the ceiling followed by the drastic movement, by its own accord, of a pewter jug. Elms and Taylor would often use the shed as a shop and sell garden implements and fertilisers to other allotment holders. These tools of the trade would become

A poltergeist was said to have once pestered a Bromley allotment! (Illustration by E. Rodrigo)

the focus for an unseen entity that began to remove the tops of bottles, and more ominously, use certain garden tools as weapons. Both men were the target of this troublesome spirit, on one occasion Mr Taylor was hit on the head by a whole box of gardening utensils, but it was Mr Elms who seemed to be the main target for the aggression. On other occasions there were strange showers of matches and soil until eventually Mr Elms, sick of the episodes, attempted an exorcism. His ritual, however, only made matters worse. Two members of the Society of Psychical Research twice visited the allotment and witnessed the activity. The invisible presence seemed to attempt some type of communication to the witnesses using the fertiliser in an effort to spell out words. On one occasion the numbers 1659 appeared on a wooden panel as if suggesting some type of date. Whilst, at other times, symbols resembling a cross and on a separate occasion, a skull, had appeared.

The alleged poltergeist activity was reported on in several newspapers, and one of the psychic investigators, a chap named Manfred Cassirer, eventually wrote a small booklet on the strangeness. On one occasion, Manfred reported that he and fellow investigator Pauline Runnalls were having a cup of tea outside the shed – so as to avoid any contamination from the fertiliser in the drink – when one of the beakers placed on the bonnet of a car began to move. This was the one episode that convinced the researchers that something uncanny was afoot. During another episode, holiday money belonging to Mr Elms had vanished and so Pauline Runnalls, in an attempt to prove the existence of the spirit, asked it if it could return the money and with that two coins sprang from nowhere, both of which struck her on the head.

The word poltergeist is said to derive from the German poltern – meaning 'to rumble' – and geist – meaning ghost. Such a spirit is rarely, if at all, seen, but is said to cause considerable disturbance, usually in homes, by throwing objects, stacking up furniture, and on some rare occasions, causing scratch marks on the flesh of people involved. An allotment shed is probably the last place anyone would expect a ghost to focus its spite, but researchers believe that such spirits have a deep connection to the psyche of the witnesses rather than to the location.

Like so many reputed poltergeist cases, the allotment activity ceased as quickly as it had begun. In his booklet, Cassirer writes, 'We do not know for certain how these phenomena start. We have on several occasions blamed an unspecified agency, whose life-span is of limited duration and whose range is closely prescribed, interacting between its victims and their domain of activity.'

Sceptics at the time argued that the men had performed an elaborate hoax, but this possibility was dismissed by the researchers when they experienced the moving beaker and the appearance of the coins. Why that particular poltergeist chose that shed and those 'victims' we will probably never know, but those involved in the case were convinced of its authenticity.

A poltergeist was also said to have manifested itself in the cellar of a property at Pinewood Road in Bromley. The couple who lived there, a Mr and Mrs Goose, reported several strange happenings with Mr Ron Goose often the main focus of the activity. The couple moved into the nineteenth-century property in 1977 and discovered that things were happening in the cellar. On one occasion Ron reported how a nail dropped from nowhere onto his foot, then on another occasion a piece of steel wall dropped onto the bench next to him. Ron would also find bent drill bits in the cellar, but weirdest of all there was the incident when Mr Goose felt as though someone had kicked him in the leg. Couple this with the strange episode when Ron dropped a tack on the floor and when he bent down to pick it up it had turned into a razor blade! Eventually the couple decided to call in a medium who blessed the house. Rita Goose commented at the time, 'When she [the medium] arrived my husband and I took her to the cellar. She said a few words and then blew in the air. About a couple of days later Ron was in the cellar and felt something or someone blow in his face. Since then – nothing!'

Ghosts in uniform

One particularly ghost-infested area of Bromley seems to be Chatterton Road. A local website called *Your County* featured a handful of brief reports of ghosts from this area. A Mr Wellens from Battle in East Sussex stated that whilst refurbishing a shop on the mentioned stretch of road, a work colleague had reported seeing the spectre of a man dressed in RAF uniform. Mr Wellens was sceptical of the incident, adding, 'We did rip it out of him but he stuck to his story.' It seems that the witness was right to stick to his story. Another chap named Peter came forward to report, 'In the late 1980s I lived on Chatterton Road and saw a man dressed in a blue military uniform from my rented room that overlooked the street. His shoes made no sound on the pavement. Some weeks later I overheard a patron of The Chatterton Arms talking about the ghost of a serviceman often seen in the street. The description matched the man I saw exactly!'

A Bromley resident named Debbie posted that the ghosts seen in the area may have had connections to Biggin Hill (*see relevant segment*). She commented, 'I think there were men stationed here [Chatterton Road] that served at Biggin Hill.' Could this also explain the apparition seen in 1996 by an unnamed witness who reported:

> I saw something in Bromley … I was walking in Chatterton Road (midway between Bromley and Bromley Common). I had been out for a meal with two friends, I had very little to drink and it was a clear March night. I saw a man dressed in a Navy Blue uniform walk towards us on the street, the person didn't seem to look at us at all and when he passed by I felt very uncomfortable. I was so uneasy I turned my head around as soon as we had passed but he had gone, I was spooked and made my friends stop and look around. They were in conversation and took no notice when he passed us by but they had seen him. I got my leg pulled and I dropped the subject. I know what I saw and the man disappeared into thin air, I wonder could this be linked to the Biggin Hill ghosts, it must only be a few miles from Chatterton Road to Biggin Hill. I never saw anything like this again.

Chatterton Road in Bromley, haunt of uniformed ghosts.

The Bansted History website mentions another ghost in uniform. The story comes from a Marie Edwards who resided at Widmore Road, Bromley from 1947. She told how, as a child and in the company of her mother and grandmother, she'd seen the ghost of a man in uniform standing by the large mantelpiece. The ghostly gent was clean shaven and had light-coloured hair. The spectre said nothing, but made his presence known for some six weeks before Marie's grandmother finally got fed up of the lingering spirit and told him to go. He was never seen again. Interestingly however, the area of the haunting had previously been the site of a plane crash. Marie mentioned how the plane had hit two houses, and that pieces of debris from the plane were discovered in the overgrown garden when the family moved in.

As a brief addition to this segment it is worth noting that Addison Road, which joins Chatterton Road, also has a ghost story. A woman in black was once reportedly seen at a property on this road in the mid-1960s. The spirit, said to have been of evil intent, was given the name Lilian by a psychic medium who investigated the haunting. The story was reported on in the *Bromley Times* of 2 December 1966 who featured the case under the heading, '*Kentish Times* embarks on ghost-probe.' The ghost was said to have plagued a young couple who owned a shop. Thirty-year-old Frank Perry and his twenty-one-year-old wife were so spooked by the presence that the medium was called in. Mr Perry's wife had just given birth to a baby boy and was told by the medium to stay away from the haunted building.

'I am frightened by what might happen,' Mr Perry told the newspaper

Addison Road – a house on this road was haunted by a woman in black.

during early December 1966. 'I want to get rid of Lilian by this weekend.'

Mr Perry had been plagued by strange tapping noises which were investigated by a *Times* reporter who stayed the night at the house. As he switched out the lights he reported feeling uneasy in the darkness particularly as he'd settled down next to a chair said to have been frequented by the grisly ghoul. Despite being covered in four blankets, the reporter noted how cold the room was in comparison to the others and then, after a short while, there came the tapping noises.

'I followed the sound, only to discover to my relief it was the window rattling in its frame.' However, after dropping off to sleep the intrepid reporter was awoken again by a loud bang. To calm his nerves he lit a cigarette but was then startled by the sound of heavy breathing close by which suddenly stopped. The writer glanced at the chair but thankfully no spectre was present and so, with the dawn breaking, he decided to go and find Mr Perry but was then unnerved by a deep rumbling sound that seemed to emanate from somewhere in the room. Rather spooked the journalist found Mr Perry fast asleep, and so returned to the room.

'I called to Lilian,' he said, 'there was no answer. I felt a fool. 'Are you there?' I asked again.

There was no answer.

He concluded in his report, 'But the mystery still remains unsolved. At seven o'clock my heart stopped as the alarm went. And I left the shop rather faster than I had entered. It was still raining. It was certainly a good night for ghosts.'

A few more spine-tinglers!

Bromley has served up some very unusual stories over the years. Sceptics may argue that some ghostly tales can be explained by misidentification or too many witnesses returning home from the local pub, but where would we be without a few pub-related hauntings?

A majority of good ghost stories always seem to be attached to old pubs. Ye Olde Whyte Lion, with its unusual name and history, seems to be the perfect setting for a spooky wintry tale. The pub, situated in Locksbottom, and which was constructed in the seventeenth century, has a flickering log fire and creaking beams. Spencer David Smith, one-time resident of Belvedere told me in December 2012, 'My brother-in-law used to run the pub, and he always stated that the toilets were the haunt of an old lady. He and my sister-in-law whilst working in the toilets reported that the doors used to slam and lock, and that an old woman would appear.' Creepy stuff!

In 2013 a male member of staff reported to me that on one occasion he was called to an area of the pub because the motion sensors had been triggered off. However, when he investigated all he found was a

Ye Olde Whyte Lion public house.

poster on the floor that had fallen from the wall. He stated, 'There was no way the poster could have fallen and triggered the sensors because it was nowhere near them. Also, I could not explain as to how the poster was folded on the floor.'

In his book *Haunted Inns of Kent*, Roger Long speaks of a macabre discovery involving a former landlord who ran the pub in the 1960s. According to Long, the landlord unearthed the skeletal remains of a female whilst renovating the property. The skull of the woman showed the mark of where a bullet had entered the forehead. Although a rather grim find, the landlord, to add to the atmosphere of the old pub, decided to place the skull on the bar and eventually turned it into a lamp – a morbid decoration indeed. Ever since then the ghost of a woman has been reported in

the bar – could it be the same old crone said to appear in the toilets? As in the case of most haunted pubs, the resident ghoul has been blamed for the creaking floorboards; the unearthly footsteps throughout the premises; the occasional glass that flies off of a shelf; and the items that often go missing. Sadly, according to a current member of staff, the skull, which was placed in a hole in the wall, has now been plastered over.

Another haunted pub in Bromley is the Beech Tree, situated on London Road. The resident ghost, according to a report from 1989, was said to have set up shop in the dank cellar. The then landlord, Terry Linton, was of the opinion that the phantom could well have been that of a former landlord or customer whose ashes were stored behind the bar. Either way, the haunting began

The Beech Tree pub on the London Road.

when Mr Linton's wife, Jane, decided to remove the ashes and bury them in the pub garden. Since then there were numerous bumps and thuds heard in the basement. Terry took the noises very seriously, thinking at first that the pub had a burglar, but upon investigation he found no one inside the building. Things became very strange when Terry found a crate of Diet Cola in the cellar, and every bottle turned upside down within it. The perturbed landlord commented, 'There were marks on the ceiling as if someone had picked up the broom and banged it. It gave me such a shock to see it my hair was standing on end.'

After this high strangeness Mr Linton decided to dig up the ashes and put them back in the pub. Since then the pub has been free of spirit trouble.

London Road is said to have another ghost too. The United Services Club was rumoured to be the haunt of an old sea captain. His ghost was popular among customers in the 1980s. The entity was said to have spooked a man who was using the toilet. The barman at the time, a fellow named Alex Morrison, was sceptical although he did say that the building used to be the site of St Margaret's Hospital. Is a spectral patient looking for attention?

Bromley is also said to have a haunted section of railway. During the early 1990s a woman was said to have been struck by a fast-moving train and her spectre has been seen on certain nights drifting along the small section of the Bromley north line. A short distance from Bromley North station is East Street. In 1872 the Old Drill Hall was opened here, and it was used by the Bromley Volunteer Rifle Corps. When the building was later used by the local Post Office, witnesses described feeling the touch of

The United Services Club in Bromley, the haunt of an old sea captain.

The Old Drill Hall – now a pub – has a ghost.

an invisible hand on their shoulder. One witness to the ghostly presence was said to have been so petrified that their hair turned white overnight! In the 1980s a cleaner at the building named Leslie Dixon believed that the phantom was of a soldier who died after a fight with another man over a girl. The building is now a pub.

A stretch of Bromley Road is said to be haunted by a woman in old-fashioned clothing. In the late 1960s there were a handful of sightings of the ghost. She was seen wearing a long dark skirt and a white blouse. The spectre was said to have appeared during the Bank Holiday of 1967 and was seen by multiple witnesses as she glided through the traffic. One of the witnesses enquired at the local library as to whether there had been an accident in the area in the past and was startled to discover that on 2 September 1898 an eighteen-year-old woman had been killed on the Bromley Road whilst cycling

to Bromley. The woman lost control of her bike and careered into a horse and cart and was killed by being crushed to death by the dray. Although there are two Bromley Roads in the area both, over the years, have had ghostly activity attributed to them. The most haunted stretch, judging by reports in the past, seems to be the A21 leading to Bellingham.

There was once mention, back in the 1960s, of a forlorn-looking male ghost said to frequent Hayes Lane in Bromley. The spectre had been noted on the outskirts of the lane, and sporadically sighted in Hayesford Park. During the early 1900s when Hayes Lane was still a country district, a man gardening at No. 103 Hayes Lane, claimed to have seen the figure of a man emerge from out of the ground. Intriguingly, the same witness, whilst walking one day with his family ten years later, saw a similar ghost but this time at Bourne Vale, a short distance from

Hayes Lane. Bravely, the witness ran to the spot where he'd seen the wraith only to find a lingering mist which he walked through. Not far from Hayes Lane one will find Pickhurst Green. A building here, once known as Longcroft, which was demolished in the 1940s, had a reputation for being haunted. Legend claims that a phantom bride used to haunt the area. She was killed on her wedding day after a dreadful coach accident. Whether the ghostly bride-to-be was the ghost of the manor we'll never know. Meanwhile, during the Second World War there were numerous legends concerning one of the local churchyards. After severe bombing it was rumoured that some of the bodies had been disturbed to the extent that some seemed to rise to the surface. These stories spooked many local children. On one occasion a hand was seen protruding from soil!

Another Bromley story comes from the *Bromley Times* of 6 November 1964. A Peggy Martyn Clark, secretary of the Kentish Authors Group, when asked about her most vivid ghost sighting from the area responded:

> … the young couple who walk through the Chariot Wheel. They are rather oddly dressed, not that that means much today. I had a peculiar feeling as they went by the table where I sat, and turned to look at them. Her whole rig-out was of white, and he was in black and wore an extraordinary looking hat. It flopped over his ears. They paused, smiled at each other then were not there at all. I am sure that they are young things from another age, and I rather like to believe they are seeking the joys of old Simpson's Palace, a mansion that centuries ago stood thereabouts. They harm no-one, anyway.

Simpson's Place was a manor house demolished around 1870. A newspaper cutting from 1907 speaks of a ghostly woman in white said to haunt the building. The figure was seen holding a torch in one hand and on some occasions being accompanied by a phantom male dressed in black and wearing a wide-brimmed hat. Is there any connection to the story of 'the man in black' you will read shortly?

One unusual folkloric account from Bromley is recorded from the 1800s. It describes how 'a tenant of a farm, who died in the hamlet of Bromley' had previously had his house plagued by swarms of bees. So much so that the swarms had completely covered his door making the poor man a recluse. Eventually when the man died and his body removed, it was said that the swarm moved on. There were also rumours at the time that the tenant's ghost still occupied the building especially when the buzzing horde returned.

Churchills!

The Churchill Theatre can be found in Bromley's bustling High Street. The theatre, which holds almost 800 people, was opened in 1977. Five years later it was rumoured to be haunted. Seat B7 is haunted by a spectre of a man wearing a trilby hat. He made his appearance after the construction of the squash courts and was alleged to have been snapped by a photographer who was taking pictures around the time of the squash championships. Strangely, the figure in the photo is said to be holding a torch and shining it in the direction of seat B7, the seat once occupied by theatre critic H.B. Hampton, who used to frequent the seat when the theatre was known as the New Theatre.

The Churchill Theatre in Bromley's busy High Street.

Interestingly, as mentioned in the *Bromley Times* of 3 June 1982, '…the new theatre is not on the same site as the old, so has H.B.'s ghostly figure moved down the High Street?'

According to the newspaper, enquiries were made regarding the ghost at British Home Stores which occupied the spot of the old theatre, but BHS manager Michael Garson said there had been no mention of ghosts. Even so, the following week a Molly Wotton wrote in to the newspaper, stating that she used to run the canteen on the site where Costain were building British Home Stores. She reported hearing strange banging noises and seeing items move of their own accord. On another occasion Molly mentioned how, whilst washing up, she was startled by the sound of chairs scraping on a floor but when she rushed to the door to open it the sounds stopped. Eventually Molly gave the ghost a pet name, Lil. The newspaper reporter concluded that, 'On Monday I heard from Churchill general manager Sylvia Rooke. She saw an apparition twice while working at the New Theatre. Sylvia described her as middle-aged; dressed in grey, with her hair pushed back off her face … she was usually seen in the circle or by a room – the area where Molly's canteen stood!'

The phantom of Father Farnham of Bromley

Well, while the title of this segment may be a slight tongue-twister, the ghost story is one of relative obscurity. The following ghostly tale comes from 1908, the day, 3 December. The encounter involved one Revd Thomas Colson, an Anglican priest who resided at a house in London. The house was of Victorian structure, and Father Colson often shared the premises with the Bishop of Southwark. One evening both men had shared dinner and, after chatting for a few hours, the bishop decided to head off for bed, leaving Father Colson alone except for a couple of servants. A short while later, Father Colson decided he too would retire to bed and ascended the stairs to his room situated on the third floor. At 6:30 a.m. Colson awoke and visited the bathroom which meant descending the stairs to the second floor. As Father Colson took a step down he realised that at the foot of the stairs was an old man. The figure wore the attire of a cleric, a black cassock, and the figure looked straight at Colson but then vanished into thin air. Colson immediately pursued, expecting to see someone standing in a corridor hidden out of sight but his search proved fruitless.

After looking around the house Father Colson went to breakfast and upon seeing the bishop asked if there had been anyone else staying in the house the previous night, to which the bishop replied in the negative. However, the bishop soon broke the news that at 6:30 a.m. that morning a Father Farnham of Bromley had passed away. Of course Father Colson, although saddened, didn't know of Father Farnham and he soon dismissed thoughts of the strange man in the house. More than a month later however, Father Colson was appointed as the replacement for Father Farnham and, whilst on a visit to the house of a local parishioner, was drawn to a large framed photo sitting on a shelf. Father Colson enquired as to whom the elderly man was, to which the parishioner replied that it was the late Father Farnham. Father Colson almost turned white, realising this was the clergyman he'd seen back at the bishop's house!

The man in black

In the *Orpington Times* of 14 November 1991 a Lilah Shea from Orpington submitted a letter asking about a strange and possibly spectral man she had seen quite regularly in Bromley's busy High Street. According to Lilah, about four years previous she'd observed a man around Christmas time walking around the High Street. 'He was a handsome gentleman with a long nose,' she wrote. 'He wore a funny shaped hat and oddly enough, sandals. His clothes were black and he reminded me of Laurence Olivier as Richard III. He dressed in a very old fashioned style and had a weird, out of this world look about him – I think he may have been a clergyman.'

It seems that the unusual man in black had become the stuff of local legend because a week later the newspaper ran a feature stating: 'Ghostly man in black is back' after four readers had written in with their tales pertaining to the dark stranger. However, a Mrs Driscoll of Orpington was of the opinion that the man was very much alive and well and not a phantom as she'd seen him in the local Army and Navy store. Another female reader, an Erica Kennedy from Sevenoaks, also dismissed any spooky connection, adding, 'He never struck me as paranormal, though I have a very open mind about these things.'

However, just when it looked as though the mystery had a more earthly explanation, a Mr Birch of Bromley was quick to comment that the mysterious man in black had been around since the late 1960s and was often seen with a ghostly woman in white. Mr Birch's late mother had an eerie encounter with the spectre in black one afternoon. She was shutting up the shop for a few hours then she saw the man by the door. She approached to tell him that the shop would not be opening until later and the man vanished into thin air. An Elmers End resident confirmed the strangeness attached to the man in black by writing that there was a similar ghost reported in 1949, but in an office based in London.

The story of the reputedly ghostly man in black ran for a few weeks, culminating on the 19 December 1991 under the heading: 'Identity crisis over ghost man', with several more mentions of the strange man. A Helen Brighty of Bromley commented that the man was 'an eccentric dresser,' but, 'certainly not a ghost' but Lilah Shea who first started the mystery claimed she'd had a weird dream about the figure who told her in it to tell people that he resembled '… the man in the Sandeman advert.' In this 1930s commercial, advertising Sandeman Port, the figure is dressed in a long black cloak and has a large, wide-brimmed black hat perched upon his head. Weirder still, another local lady, a Margaret Kingdon of Downham, also claimed to have dreamt of the man in black, but several weeks before the newspaper story. She told *The Times* that in her dream she was in a church and was accompanied by the tall, dark stranger.

... and the not so ghostly woman in black!

A strange story comes from the *Western Mail*, from Perth (Australia) of all places, dating back to 27 October 1927. The small article, presented under the heading, 'The Ghost's Home', which I've reproduced here, speaks of a figure that was first thought to be a spectre. It described how:

Weird noises amongst the tombstones late at night, and the flitting figure of a little old woman dressed in black and carrying an umbrella, have been causing disquiet amongst people living in the vicinity of Bromley (Kent) Parish Church during

the past few weeks. Almost every night, approaching 12, the dark figure has been seen to pass through the lych-gate, glide along the path, encircle the church, and vanish into the porch.

Girls and young men employed at drapery stores overlooking the churchyard at the back, disturbed by the nightly visitations, kept watch. Each night the 'ghost' was seen to visit a certain tombstone and pause there for some time before disappearing into the church. Deciding to 'lay' the 'ghost', they scaled the wall and crept round the churchyard to the porch. Suddenly something black reared up and flapped at them. They fled.

Feeling braver in broad daylight, they returned next day and made a search of the churchyard. Behind the tombstone which the ghost was seen to visit they found a heap of rugs, blankets and a feather pillow, hidden under an old door leaning up against the tomb. To see what would happen they hid the 'ghost's' bed in a distant corner and that night kept watch again. This time the 'ghost' appeared as usual about 11 o'clock and visited the tomb, from which it roamed about as if in frantic search for its lost bed. Early next morning a quaint old woman approached the constable on duty at Market Square. She flourished an umbrella and told a tale to him of thieves who had stolen her property. She followed him to the police station and made a complaint.

There she was recognised as 75-year-old Miss Mary Squirrel, the strangest character in Bromley. For years Mary Squirrel has not had a roof over her head. She has been sleeping out of doors ever since she had a fight with the Bromley Town Council about her rates. For some time it was known that she slept in the unfinished Grand Hall in the High

Street, slipping in when the workmen knocked off at night. Then the Grand Hall was reopened and Miss Squirrel had to find a new shelter. Nobody knew that she had taken up her quarters in the porch of Bromley Parish Church except the vicar, Canon J.K. Wilson, M.A., and the verger, Mr Henry Brown.

And so, an intriguing yet solved case of mistaken identity!

The Crown & Pepper, formerly The Tiger's Head on Mason's Hill.

The one-legged soldier

In the 1950s it was rumoured that Mason's Hill, which is situated close to Bromley town centre, was the haunt of a one-legged ghostly soldier. Press reports from the spring of 1955 assert that the hopping spook had appeared in a photograph, taken years before, of some cottages which used to stand on the hill. It seems that, decades before, the local soldier had become a bit of a bogeyman with one local woman stating, 'My mother used to threaten me with "Peg-leg" if I didn't behave.' On Friday 18 March 1955 the *West Kent Mercury* front page headline read 'Ghosts haunted Mason's Hill – Bromley tales of limping steps in the night – soldier or murder victim?' after a licensee of the Tiger's Head (now the Crown & Pepper) pub had come forward to speak of the local ghost story.

Mr Joe Anthony told the newspaper that although he'd never seen the rumoured spectre he had, on several occasions after midnight, heard the limping phantom move off into the direction of Tiger Lane. He commented, 'About a year ago during the night we had a round piece of glass entirely removed from a first-storey window at the back of the house, although we missed no property. Since then I wanted to know who might be prowling about in the dead of night. So, when I have heard someone limping around in the lane or the yard I have gone out to investigate and each time have found no one.'

However, on one occasion Mr Anthony claims to have seen a figure of a man at the bottom of the yard but upon calling out received no answer. Mr Anthony was also quick to tell the newspaper that although he didn't believe in ghosts he was rather unnerved by a sound 'rather like a horse pawing on cobble stones.'

Around seventy-five or so years previous to 1955 there had been a small 'beerhouse' known as the Three Horses, which sat opposite the Tiger's Head. A chap named Thomas Partridge was landlord of the Three Horses and was arrested for the murder of a young woman who went missing after visiting the pub. Her hat was discovered in a well that was situated in the grounds of the Tiger's Head. Even so, this macabre incident does not explain the sound of the horse or the limping ghost.

2

SHIVERS AT SHORTLANDS

Just a mile from Bromley sits the ward of Shortlands. The area was once known as Clay Hill, but became Shortlands around 1800. The name is said to be of medieval origination, concerning the fields that lined the valley which the River Ravensbourne wormed its way through. The fields were said to lack width, hence the name Shortlands. Oliver Cromwell's skull was once reputed to have been stored at an old country house at Shortlands in the 1850s.

The phantom highwayman

No book on Kent ghosts would be complete without a tale pertaining to a darkly clad spectral highwayman. One such phantom was said to haunt a stretch of Kingswood Road and was last seen in the late 1920s. One May, a young girl had gone out with her mother to post a letter. As they approached the postbox the girl suddenly noticed a dark shape moving across the fields in the distance. The object appeared at first to be a cloud as it travelled from what was once known as Kingswood House to Kingswood Road. The girl stood agog, but then noticed that her mother could also see the black shape which was almost upon them, and then in a blur passing them. In 1972 the girl, by this time a middle-aged woman told the *Bromley Times*, '…as it passed us, we saw to our great astonishment the clearly-defined upper parts of a horse – as if seen above the top of a high hedge – bearing a rider on its back who wore the traditional tricorne hat,

Kingswood Road – haunted by a phantom highwayman on horseback.

and the hair in a queue. The apparition had no legs and made not the slightest sound. It raced away, across the pavement and disappeared into the fence of what was then Oak Lodge, home of the Darrell family…'

According to the witness the spectre had also been seen at the time by a Mr Portman, coachman to the Wilson family, who resided at the long-since demolished Woodside.

May's Hill Road at Shortlands.

Mystery at May's Hill Lodge

The *Newsshopper* of 28 July 1999 asked if anyone knew of the mysterious history attached to May's Hill Lodge after sisters Mandy Frumosu and Vanessa Marton had reported restless spirits in their Shortlands home for several years. According to this newspaper, 'Vanessa, and sister Mandy, have owned a flat within May's Hill Lodge for 10 years.' The ghostly disturbances began with a series of knocking noises in one of the bedrooms. On another occasion Mandy reported the feeling of being watched one evening whilst brushing her hair in the hallway. She said, 'I presumed it was my dad who had been in the flat with me. Then, I felt someone touch my arm. There was no one there; and my dad had been nowhere near me at the time.'

Shortly afterwards Vanessa had a strange experience whilst watching television with her boyfriend Jim. After settling down she heard someone whisper 'Ness' into her ear.

Could the ghost have been that of a woman named Nellie who used to live at the flat?

3

HAUNTING AT BIGGIN HILL

Do things go bump at Biggin Hill?

According to researcher John Nelson, just over a century ago Biggin Hill could not be found on any map. At the time, the area was simply farmland, but much has changed over the years. Originally the area was known as Aperfield and part of the Cudham parish. Biggin Hill was best known for its RAF airfield, this area is now occupied mostly by the London Biggin Hill airport. During the Second World War Biggin Hill airfield played a huge part in securing defences against the enemy. The area is also considered one of Kent's most haunted locations and you're about to read why.

Phantoms of land and air

Over the years there have been so many alleged sightings of ghostly air personnel, and phantom planes around Biggin Hill that the tales have become somewhat humdrum. Local researcher Bob Ogley wrote a fascinating book about the history of Biggin Hill, and covered a great deal of the ghost stories. The most well-known spectre of the airfield is said to be a ghostly Spitfire plane, and those privileged to have experienced the anomaly report how they hear the sound of the Merlin engines whirring in the distance and yet the plane never appears. On occasion witnesses also claim to see a plane that dissolves into thin air. In 1994 an issue of the *Kent Messenger* reported on the ghost, stating: 'People living near the famous Battle of Britain airfield at Biggin Hill, Kent, have often reported the sound of a wartime Spitfire returning home from a sortie. Occasionally the plane has actually been seen, screaming low towards the landing strip, then turning into a victory roll before disappearing as mysteriously as it has appeared.'

In his 1985 book *Ghosts of Kent*, ghost-hunter Peter Underwood confirms the classic haunting stating,

> Those who live around the airfield say there is no mistaking the sound of a Spitfire screaming in to land and it is largely residents and people who know about such things who are the witnesses for these ghostly sounds. The date of 19 January is, I am told, when the sounds are most often heard. Some say the long-dead pilot signals his return with a low victory roll before coming in to land; others say that men's voices are heard, glasses clink together and sounds are heard that would have followed the return of a victorious RAF pilot forty years ago.

A majority of the ghosts observed around Biggin Hill appear to be what are known as recorded spirits – ghosts

A spectral Spitfire is said to haunt the skies over Biggin Hill. This plane situated outside the chapel stands as a memorial to all Spitfire squadrons who operated from the airfield during the Second World War.

embedded in a moment of time only to be replayed back to witnesses who could be deemed sensitive enough to see them. One such account took place in 1963 and involved a van driver man named Mr Levy who at 3 a.m. was delivering newspapers when he spotted a man standing by the side of the road up ahead. What struck Mr Levy most about the figure was the fact the gentleman in question was dressed in full airman regalia. The airman appeared to be flagging Mr Levy down but as he got closer the man seemed to vanish. At first the witness thought he'd run the pilot down but there was no sign of the gentleman. A local policeman was of the opinion that the ghostly figure had been that of a Flight Lieutenant whose plane crashed into the hillside decades before. Another road encounter took place in 1958 and involved a chap named Les Lyne who, with a friend, spotted a ghostly figure adorned in white which emerged from a hedge and crossed the road ahead. The men did not stick around to see if the figure vanished, so petrified were they by its appearance.

A number of phantom airmen have been seen alongside some of Biggin Hill's more quiet lanes. Spectral airmen have also been seen at Hayes Common and in some of the houses now built on the site of the old airfield. In 1972 a Mr and Mrs Harrison moved into a bungalow at Hawthorne Avenue which is close to Biggin Hill cemetery. One evening Mrs Harrison claimed to have encountered a ghostly airman in one of the rooms of the building. The ghost appeared but seemed to be accompanied by a strange thudding noise and manly voices. Only after some research did the woman find out that the haunted room in question had once been some type of rest room for pilots and that the dull thudding noises may well have been coming from the darts they were throwing.

A ghostly airman. (Illustration by E. Rodrigo)

Plaque at Biggin Hill.

On Friday 29 September 2011 author Bob Ogley, in writing for *This Is Kent* spoke of another ghost sighting, this time made by a motorist who at the time was driving towards Keston. According to Bob, at the time of the encounter – which occurred past midnight – it had been snowing lightly. The motorist in question, a man named Austin O'Malley, had been driving by the open section of the airfield when he was alerted to a figure standing on the side of the hill and looking across the valley. Mr O'Malley told Bob, 'I slowed down, hooted and flashed him twice. I thought he was an airman, either lost or drunk so I stopped the car, crossed the road and called out to him. He didn't turn his head. He simply zipped up his uniform and walked slowly down the hill.'

Had this simply been a flesh and blood man, out of place with the surroundings or one of those elusive ghostly pilots reported every now and then around the airfield? Ghosts of the Women's Auxiliary Air Force are also presumed to haunt Biggin Hill. Vincent Square, situated near the A233, off Leaves Green Road, was the scene for an unusual ghost encounter. In the 1980s people residing at the houses nearby reported strange feelings of unease and the occasional peculiar, inexplicable noise but the most stirring incident involved members of the Navy, Army and Air Force Institute. One evening the NAAFI women were standing, chatting in the car park when they suddenly saw the top halves of a group of women from the Auxiliary Air Force who slowly faded from view.

Another ghost said to haunt Biggin Hill appeared, albeit very briefly, in the chapel of St George's which can be found on the main road. According to researcher Bob Ogley, more than 450 aircrew, all of

Vincent Square is reputed to be haunted by ghosts of the Women's Auxiliary Air Forces.

The chapel of St George's at Biggin Hill.

whom perished whilst flying from Biggin Hill between 1939 and 1945, have their names inscribed on the oaken panel (reredos) inside the chapel. One afternoon retired Wing Commander David Duval, who'd been supervising any updates and refurbishment of the panel, had a visitor to the chapel. A scruffy-looking man enquired to David about a Wing Commander Slater who he could not find on the reredos. Mr Duval pointed the name out on the board and then left the rather unkempt man to his own devices. However, when Mr Duval returned there was no sign of the gent. This was rather odd because the door to the chapel would always give off an annoying squeak when someone entered or exited the building. Stranger still, other staff had met the dishevelled man only to find him gone when they returned from attempting to

answer his query. Each time the man left the building a weird cold spot had formed in the chapel. As if things could not get any stranger, when one of the chapel caretakers observed the board to look for the mentioned Wing Commander Slater, he was shocked to find that the name had in fact been omitted. According to Bob Ogley, 'David Duval could not believe that such a major error had been missed by three people who had checked the board.' Immediately the error was rectified and the strange man was never seen again. Is it possible the elusive figure had been the spectre, or at least a spectral friend or relative, of Wing Commander Slater?

Interestingly, when I visited the chapel in February 2013 I spoke to a gentleman who works there who told me that Wing Commander Slater's name had not been omitted from the reredos but certain details of his rank may well have been and this may have upset the mysterious visitor. The gentleman also mentioned briefly that a handful of years ago a colleague of his, whilst working in the chapel, had seen the figure of a man dressed in RAF Uniform who had walked by the curtained entrance to the altar. The witness attempted to put the 'ghost' down to a trick of the eye but was convinced the figure had worn specific attire. However, when he searched the chapel, there was no one else around.

Bob Ogley also wrote of the woman who, whilst walking down Polesteeple Hill to the Grove a few years ago, noticed how the atmosphere had dramatically changed and there was a sudden drop in temperature. The chilly air seemed to spook her two dogs who froze on the spot. Days later the woman returned to the area and had a weirder encounter. Upon returning to the Grove her dogs suddenly disappeared. She reported, 'I had this feeling I was being enclosed by arms. Someone was drawing me close and I actually saw a cloak being placed around me. Then a voice said quietly: "Don't be afraid." And the cloak opened revealing the dogs.'

In the 1940s a Messerschmitt 109 crashed in the woods near to the Grove. Is it possible the pilot still haunts the area?

Inside the chapel at Biggin Hill.

Animals, especially domestic cats and dogs, are believed to sense the presence of ghosts. According to Bob Ogley in 1948 a man named Ken, who was stationed in 'a large house near the South Camp not far from the main road to Bromley,' had an eerie experience which involved his Alsatian dog. One night whilst alone in his billet, Ken noticed his dog had become rather agitated. The animal then sprang to its feet and ran to the kitchen and began to bark at a section of blank wall. Ken was intrigued by this behaviour and so made a few enquiries. He discovered that the particular section of room that was once attached to the kitchen had been used as a meat store. It was in this room that a Polish airman had hung himself. The storeroom would have been situated behind the wall that Ken's dog had been barking at. In 1995 a woman named Nicole, who lived with her husband Keith in one of the caravans in the region of the redeveloped North Camp, had a spooky encounter which again involved a pet. As dusk began to draw in her dog began to growl and bark. Nicole was surprised to see the figure of a man dressed in RAF uniform walking towards the back of the nearby houses. When questioned as to why he was loitering around the site he suddenly disappeared.

The ghosts said to haunt the Biggin Hill area are clearly in no rush to move on. The airfield may indeed be the place these lost souls were last happiest.

Nearby apparitions

Just two miles from Biggin Hill sits the village of Leaves Green. This delightfully named place has a haunted pub. The Crown Inn can be found on the

Leaves Green Road on the A233. During the Battle of Britain, British airmen would frequent the pub. The ghost however is not one of these brave pilots, instead, the spectre is said to be that of a miner who in 1896 died after a terrible accident in a nearby chalk mine. His body was taken to the inn and it seems as if his lost soul has never left.

Close by to Leaves Green is Keston. This part rural, part suburban area sits on the edge of Hayes Common. On 6 May 1981 three schoolgirls had a terrifying encounter in the vicinity of Keston Ponds. A figure, clad in a dark cloak and wearing a black pointed hat, was seen to be hovering over one of the three ponds in the area. The entity appeared to be wearing a belt of glowing lights around its waist. Despite this being a very peculiar encounter little appears on record about this creepy confrontation.

The eleven-mile River Ravensbourne rises at Keston Ponds in a spot known

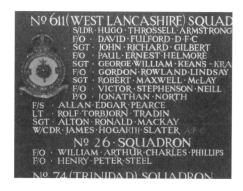

The name of Wing Commander Slater can be seen on the reredos within the chapel at Biggin Hill airfield.

as Caesar's Well. The legend here is that when Caesar's legions marched towards London they were directed to this well by ravens to quench their thirst. The well is said to have healing powers. Some people have reported their own creepy encounters with ghostly Roman soldiers in the area, although sightings seem rare.

The Crown Inn on the Leaves Green Road.

4

SPOOKS AROUND BECKENHAM

The town of Beckenham can be found less than two miles west of Bromley town. The Domesday Book of 1086 refers to the town as Bacheham. The name of the town derives from 'a village on the stream.' In 1878 the town was hit by severe flooding. Bizarrely, from 1686 to 1689 Beckenham suffered from plagues of hedgehogs! More than a century ago Beckenham existed as a village, but today has a population of more than 80,000. One of its inhabitants was William Pring, a notorious highwayman. Some of its inhabitants however, seem to be of the ghostly kind!

Things that go bump in the park

A majority of people whether interested or sceptical of spirit forms, will often argue that there's no substantial evidence for their existence. However, on the rare occasion when a sample of evidence is put forward, it is often dismissed. Even so, on Thursday 13 May 2010 the *News Shopper* online reported: 'Dog walker spots "ghost"

in Kelsey Park' after a local man named Paul Reed claimed to have photographed an anomaly at Beckenham. Mr Reed had been photographing his Border Collie in the park one afternoon when suddenly his dog froze on the spot. Mr Reed thought that his dog may have simply had an off day until he returned home and uploaded his photographs to his computer. In one of the photographs – shown by the newspaper – there appeared to be a figure standing near some bushes.

Mr Reed looked at the photo and noticed what appeared to be the shape of a transparent woman in Victorian style attire, although he remained on the fence with his opinion, telling the newspaper, 'It could just have been the sunlight reflected on the bushes, but some people are saying it's really spooky.'

The jury is out regarding what the photograph shows but Mr Reed couldn't explain the behaviour of his dog, adding, 'It was definitely odd, he wasn't his usual self. He was cowering back towards me.'

In the summer of 1976 a Mr Harris claimed to have had a supernatural

Kelsey Park in Beckenham.

encounter in the area of Beckenham Common. At the time Mr Harris had been repairing a stairwell at a local veterinary clinic and by the time he'd finished work it had been evening time. After finishing up he decided to grab a takeaway in the local High Street before making his way home. Mr Harris walked alongside St George's Church and then decided as a shortcut to stroll through the church grounds. Although the town had been busy this route was far more peaceful in the dusk. Upon reaching the front of the church Mr Harris heard the sound of women laughing, and so decided to take this route home, drawn by the merriment. As he rounded the bend he noticed two women up ahead, they were positioned near the rear of the church. Mr Harris approached, and noticed that both women were dressed in long gowns, but the bottom half of their bodies appeared to be misty rather than detailed. The women were relatively young and seemed to have an uncanny air about them.

Spontaneously Mr Harris blurted out, 'Hello, how you doing?' and the women, not fazed by the appearance of Mr Harris casually looked at him, smiled, and then continued their jolly conversation. Mr Harris stood and watched as the women laughed, but then to his astonishment they began to fade from view and then were nowhere to be seen. Mr Harris acted quickly, moving to the exact spot where the women had been standing but there was no sign of them. Indeed there was not even a trace of the women, no impression in the ground and no disturbance of the foliage.

St George's Church in Beckenham looms over the treetops.

Mr Harris was dumbstruck, but unable to explain as to where the women had gone and so rather perplexed, hastily made his way home.

... and more!

Beckenham has long been known for its ghost stories. Many years ago a teenager named James had a bizarre experience whilst staying at the house of a relative in Queens Road. James woke in the middle of the night to use the toilet but as he turned toward the lavatory a figure of a man, who appeared to be on fire, ran towards him and quick as a flash disappeared. The apparition was only in view for a few seconds. James screamed in terror, waking the rest of the inhabitants up who rushed to his aid. There were no further sightings of the fiery phantom but James was told by his aunt, that when she was young she saw the spectre of an old lady in the same area where the burning man had been seen. James conducted further research into the area and found out that on the land at the rear of the property used to sit several houses but these were bombed in the war. Had James seen one of the victims of a bombing raid?

There is another story concerning an alleged haunted house, this time dating back to the 1960s. The *Victoria Advocate* newspaper of 24 March 1963 reported: 'Galloping family ghost returns to old haunts', with mention of a spectral coach and horses, seen around the cottage of the Betts family. According to the newspaper, the ghost was said to have appeared as 'a phantom coachman driving four proud horses.' The apparition had plagued the family for some time, with owner Albert Betts reporting, 'We were sitting in the upper room and my wife had given little Joey her cup of cocoa when we heard it ...'

A ghostly coach and horses in full flight. (Illustration by E. Rodrigo)

The phantom coach and four horses scared Joey so much she spilled her hot beverage down her pyjamas. However, the most intriguing aspect about the haunting was the fact that one night, the Betts' dog, Cindy, had fallen ill, and so she was taken to the animal sanatorium some twenty miles away in Ilford. At midnight that night, a man named Reg Filmer had been walking his dog in the area when he heard the ghostly coach and its equally phantasmal horses. He commented, 'I heard the noise of horses and wheels. It got closer and closer, but I could see nothing.'

Although, while Cindy was away from the house, the Betts enjoyed a peaceful night the ghost would once again wish to make itself known. Indeed a while later Mr Betts revealed that, '… there was a bump in the night. I saw our ghost crashing through the greenhouse … he ruined my chrysanthemums.'

There is also a brief legend pertaining to a spectral white horse once said to have haunted a meadow near Pickhurst Hill. The ghost, complete with phantom mount, has also been reported on the road from Pickhurst Hill to Beckenham.

Another haunted Beckenham property is recorded from the early 1930s and involved a Mrs Jona. One night she woke and on turning over, was startled to see the figure of a large woman sitting in the bedside chair. The ghost was scowling at Mrs Jona who immediately roused her husband from his slumber. He too saw the spectre, but as he climbed out of bed and approached it the figure faded. Mrs Jona asked her doctor if he knew anything of the previous tenants and was amazed when he mentioned that a large woman used to live in the house with her husband but had died in the room directly below Mr and Mrs Jona's bedroom. Another weird story comes from the files of journalist William Thomas Stead who once wrote of a woman who resided in Essex but for a short while had stayed with family in Beckenham. The woman's husband had remained in Essex as part of a shooting party, but one afternoon whilst upstairs she had a strange vision of her husband. She sensed that he was outside the house and so looked out of the window and was amazed to see him coming through the garden gate of the Beckenham property.

The woman bolted downstairs, shouting to her sister-in-law, 'Why, there's Tom!' but upon opening the front door there was no sign of her husband. Bizarrely, what the woman didn't realise was that at the exact same time of seeing her 'husband' enter the gate, he had been shot in Essex and fainted from the pain. Thankfully, Tom was only injured, but why had his spirit seemingly appeared several miles away – especially as he hadn't perished from the gunshot wound?

Beckenham (Stone Park) Hospital, now demolished – like so many hospitals across the country – is said to be haunted. The legend is that a grey lady often glides out of the matron's office and slips along the corridor. The ghost then appears to walk as if ascending a flight of invisible stairs before vanishing. Those who have seen her describe the figure as wearing a long grey cloak and being quite tall in stature. Interestingly, in the 1980s several workmen uncovered a hidden staircase in the exact area where the spectre walks. The concealed staircase would have led to the Harry Lyne Ward, which was the oldest ward in the hospital. Local teenagers often like to keep one of the hospital ghost stories alive. They tell the macabre tale of how a young woman died whilst giving birth

in the hospital and now she haunts the land where the hospital used to sit.

Before the hospital was demolished security guards patrolling the empty building often reported having frightening experiences. Some of these were mentioned in the *Bromley Advertiser* of 3 September 1987 under the front-page heading: 'Guards get the jitters!' According to the report, managing director of Syd Bishop and Sons Demolition, a Mr David Bishop said: 'Some of my men have said, "I don't like to go in there boss."'

This came after claims that the eerie-looking white building, which operated as a maternity hospital up until 1985, had been haunted by peculiar cries, reported by staff watching over the site before demolition. A spokesperson for Bromley Health Authority was sceptical in regards to the reputed ghosts stating, 'I think you should tell the security men that the screams could be coming from neighbouring properties and not from a ghost!'

A ghost story was once attached to a stretch of road that used to run alongside what was known as the Lazy Toad pub. The spectre was said to be that of a young woman, dressed in summery clothing (even in the winter months) that would be seen to disappear before the eyes of witnesses. One witness, a woman named Jackie Martin claimed that the ghostly female looked as if she was in her late teens and wearing attire that suggested she was from the 1980s. The *Newshopper* of 4 June 1997 covered the ghost story, stating 'Experts in the paranormal are queuing up to investigate a sighting of an "unhappy looking" mystery girl outside a Beckenham pub.'

Richard Read, the then manager of the pub commented that he'd always heard the rumours about a phantom girl. The report also claimed that Revd Peter

Thomas, a 'Diocesan paranormal expert …' would be contacting the pub to conduct an investigation.

In the winter of 2012 I spoke to a Malcolm Hayes who told me of a brief ghost story from Beckenham. He stated,

I'm an Orpington (Petts Wood born) lad but I can only recall one ghost story which my uncle Derek used to recount at Christmas time (which incidentally often used to scare the Christmas pud' out of me!). Apologies for any vagueness in the story because it's around fifty years since I last heard it. At the time, in the 1950-'60s, he was a police station sergeant somewhere in the Tower Bridge area and for some reason (maybe shortages of staff or temporary secondment?) he had to send two constables to somewhere in our (Bromley – maybe Beckenham) area because a young mother alone in her flat with a young child had reported a loft hatch opening and closing. Thinking it was an intruder he sent two of his burliest Bobbies round but they could find nothing in the flat or loft and were about to leave having assured the family that all was well. But the child's screaming brought the constables pounding back into the boy's bedroom where the loft hatch was opening and closing all by itself. My uncle said that the burliest of the policeman had tackled many violent incidents of a physical nature with no problem at all but when he brought the family back to the police station – because neither they (nor the policemen) would stay there any longer – he was white and shaking. It was something beyond the understanding of them all and fear of the unknown is the worst I guess. My uncle was not a man to make things up and he always maintained it was absolutely true – and that made it all the creepier for us kids at family gatherings.

Kent House is a railway station situated between Beckenham and Penge. The station, formerly known as Kent House (Beckenham) gets its name from the Kent House farm which used to be situated nearby. The house was considered the oldest in Kent and before being demolished was said to be haunted by a woman. Little is known about the spectre but it could well have been the spirit of a lady who was murdered in the house during the early sixteenth century.

Beckenham beasts

The realm of the paranormal seems to have no boundaries. All manner of anomalies exist within its murky fold, ranging from spectral vehicles, to eerie lights. For me, however, one of the most intriguing aspects of the supernatural has to be the phenomenon of ghastly, ghostly animals.

One of the most bizarre and seemingly supernatural experiences to have taken place in Beckenham isn't confined to the foggy realms of folklore, but to more modern times. During the festive season of 2011 a man named Peter Butler had been participating in a nightly vigil at a park in Beckenham. He'd heard of many stories regarding the ghosts of the area, and was drawn to an old tree in the vicinity which over the years had been given the reputation of being a hanging tree. Peter was armed with his video camera and in the gloom had been panning across the park when he became aware of an apparition staring at him from the vicinity of a children's play area. Peter focused his camera on the object. The figure, which resembled an animal with two glowing eyes, was perched on one of the playground structures and then leapt off into the bushes.

The story was investigated in 2012 by the paranormal television show *Fact or Faked* who sent a team of experts all the way from the United States to Beckenham in search of answers. The team was headed by former FBI agent Ben Hansen, who was accompanied by journalist Jael de Pardo, tech specialist Devin Marble and monster-hunter Josh Gates of *Destination Truth* fame. Peter, who showed the footage to the team stated, 'At first I thought it was a person, it was about 4½ft, but I guess the closest thing I could compare it to would be a monkey.' The video shows a figure, hunched over and peering from the top of a playground structure. As it leaps off into the darkness a lengthy tail is evident.

The team spent the night in the park, re-enacting various scenarios with the possibility of explaining the footage. At one point Devin adorns himself in chain mail, and armed with a plastic sword climbs to the top of the playground structure and is filmed leaping from it into the darkness. Witness Peter claimed that there was a possibility that someone had dressed up in chainmail and hoaxed him. This seemed to make some sense considering that Chislehurst Caves isn't that far away from Beckenham. Had somebody been involved in a medieval re-enactment at the caves and for some unknown reason wandered into the park to spook a passer-by? The team didn't seem convinced and so decided on plan B; being the possibility that the anomaly on the video was in fact some sort of wild animal that had escaped from a zoo or private menagerie.

Fact or Faked enlisted the help of a wild animal handler named Chris Brown, who brought with him to the park a ring-tailed lemur (*Lemur catta*). Such a creature normally inhabits the wilds of Madagascar but as Chris stated, such animals were popular in zoo parks across the world with a few hundred being kept in the United Kingdom. The ring-tailed lemur belongs to the suborder of primate known as Strepsirhini. These agile creatures have distinctive ringed tails which can measure up to 2ft in length. They have a reflective layer to the eye which enables them to hunt at night, but they only stand around 18in in height. This seemed to contradict with the height of the creature which Peter filmed. Despite the investigative team reconstructing the scene employing the lemur, the animal failed to live up to expectations. Although its eyes reflected in the night, the animal was clearly too small to match the size of the apparition in the video. The team then moved on to a third option, the possibility of a hoax. They built a model in the hope of matching the form on the film, but failed miserably and so decided to conduct a nightly vigil, armed with infra-red cameras and the like. Despite the usual modern-day ghost-hunting shenanigans, including rustling bushes and misinterpretation of natural wildlife, the team found no evidence of paranormal activity or roaming monsters.

Interestingly, Beckenham Place Park also had a 'monster' scare. The park, which can be found straddling the Lewisham and Bromley border made the headlines in 2000 when several witnesses, including local golfers, came forward to report they'd seen a 'phantom kangaroo' on the loose! The *Guardian* newspaper dubbed the creature the 'beast of Beckenham' and stated that the 6ft tall animal had left footprints in the soil. These were analysed by experts at the Natural History Museum who apparently stated that the impressions were made by a creature that was bigger than a dog. Richard Rose, a spokesperson for Lewisham council commented that, 'There have been several sightings of this kangaroo and we suspect it may have escaped from a zoo.'

The main problem with this theory however was the fact that no zoo parks had lost any of its marsupials, and a creature as large as a kangaroo would have literally stuck out like a sore thumb. Yet, like so many similar stories to make the headlines, such a beast was never found. Had the creature been some type of apparition?

A few researchers at the time, including myself and members of the RSPCA, put forward the theory that the animal had in fact been a wallaby. Wallabies had been kept in the past on farms throughout England and many escaped, especially during the severe storm of 1987 which battered Kent. Although a wallaby resembles a kangaroo, it only stands around 2ft in height whereas a red kangaroo measures over 5ft in height. Golf club barman Michael Johnson was keen to cash in on the unusual sightings, stating, 'We are hoping it could be something of a local Loch Ness monster, it's been great publicity for the golf club.'

Sadly the mystery fizzled out as there were no further sightings of the mystery animal, so had it been a phantom after all?

Spook lights

In the summer of 2010 several Beckenham residents came forward to report a number of unidentified flying objects in the skies of the town. The cluster of sightings caused a minor panic with the *Newsshopper* receiving seven phone calls in just one day from frightened locals. One witness, a woman named Elaine Perkins told the newspaper, 'I just could not understand what they were, I have never seen anything like it,' whilst an Olive Jackson from Orpington commented, 'It looked like they had taken off and then slowed down.'

Despite the mild hysteria the strange orange lights proved to be nothing more than Chinese lanterns – often set off by people having summer barbeques and parties. The lanterns are lit, and give off an orange glow as they soar into the air. After a few minutes the flame dissipates and the lanterns fade into darkness.

So, little green men were not haunting the skies over Beckenham, but spook lights of an unknown nature have embedded themselves into ghost lore for centuries. Such lights, also known as ghost lights, or will-o'-the-wisp are often associated with foggy marshes, and are said to appear as small, bright lights of varying colour. Should anyone spot a spook light and follow it, the legend claims that the pursuer will be led to their death. Ghost lights have never been fully explained, in other instances such manifestations are known as ball lightning which has been known to occur during severe thunderstorms. These fiery orbs, which vary in size and colour, have appeared in people's houses and make their presence known by an eerie crackling noise. These lights have been seen to explode or exit a building via an open window or door. Centuries ago when such phenomena were recorded, they were deemed as supernatural and demonic entities, blamed for causing terrible fires in churches. Weird balls of light cross over into several paranormal categories, such as the UFO phenomenon, although there is no evidence whatsoever to suggest that such bizarre forms are of alien origin. Over the last few decades, and particularly since the advent of digital cameras, these odd glowing balls have become known as orbs. Some ghost hunters and paranormal investigators believe that orbs are the first sign of a spirit form, although sceptics argue that such manifestations are nothing more than particles of dust and moisture distorted by the camera. It is very likely that orbs are a natural phenomenon akin to the already mentioned will-o'-the-wisp, but not all of these materialisations can be rationally explained.

Author and Fortean researcher Nick Redfern told me of a queer encounter involving a spook light at Beckenham that occurred a few decades ago and is recorded in the National Archives. He stated, 'Midway through 1963, an event occurred at Beckenham, Kent, that bore all the hallmarks of an encounter with one of the fabled Foo Fighters of the Second World War [Author note: Foo Fighters were strange balls of light that seemed to display some sort of intelligence and were reported as buzzing aircraft pilots]. And, the witness had a military background: he had served during the hostilities of 1939- 45 with an anti-aircraft detachment and until 1961 was attached to a territorial unit of the British Army.'

According to Nick, the witness, a Mr W. Hooper had informed the Air Ministry that 'At 0150 hrs on Tuesday the 27th August I was awakened by my wife to see what appeared to be something in flames falling from the sky, slightly N.W. of my house. This object appeared to be a ball of incandescent gas, red and black and was about a foot in diameter, and gave the impression of intense heat. It dropped like a stone from approximately 1000ft to 500ft, then stayed still for about 2-3 seconds, then started moving at an incredible speed in a Northerly direction and was out of sight in a matter of about 4 seconds. As it went away the wind brought a slight humming sound to us and the red and black appearance turned slightly yellow.'

Mr Hooper added, 'I would be grateful if you could throw any light on the matter for me and would like especially to know if you had anything showing on your radar screens at the time I have stated. I am convinced that the object was powered as it travelled against the wind, and think what we saw may have been some sort of exhaust gas or flame.'

Nick added that, 'Possibly anticipating that Whitehall would offer a totally down-to-earth explanation for what occurred, Mr Hooper closed his letter thus: "I hope you will not try and persuade me that the object was a meteorological balloon as these as far as I know could not possibly travel against the wind".'

Nick concluded, 'In this particular case, Air Intelligence once again asserted that a solution had been found. Mr Hooper, came back the conclusion, had been fooled by a "fireball". That the UFO had hovered in the air for two to three seconds was ignored by Air Intelligence; as was the fact that Mr Hooper's anti-aircraft work during the Second World War would have given him first-class observational skills.'

We'll never know exactly what Mr Hooper observed in 1963, or whether such a light was ghostly or extraterrestrial, but one thing is for sure, this had been an unnerving experience involving a man not prone to hallucination or misidentification.

5

ORPINGTON ODDITIES

In the year 1036 the town of Orpington was recorded as Orpedingetune. Chronicler Edward Hasted records that the name Orpington is a corruption of Dorpentune, meaning village or street where a spring rises. The Domesday Book of 1086 recorded that less than 100 people inhabit Orpington. Today more than 15,000 people live in the suburban town. At Crofton sits a Roman villa, which was discovered in 1926 by workmen. During the Second World War parts of Orpington were heavily bombed.

Weird tales aplenty

One of the queerest stories to emerge from Orpington folklore concerns the phantom hair-clipper, an elusive individual who accosted young women in the early 1900s. Charles Fort, in his work *Wild Talents* speaks of a seventeen-year-old lady named Dorris Whiting, who one evening whilst approaching her home noticed a man leaning on the garden gate. As Dorris passed the suspicious man he grabbed hold of her hair and cut a chunk off before running away. Dorris screamed in terror and her father and brother ran to her aid, but despite a thorough search of the immediate area they could find no trace of the assailant. It is also recorded that another young woman, employed as a maid at Crofton Hall, suffered the same unusual attack. Whether it was around the same time we do not know, but Fort mentions how the girl, who worked for a Mrs Glanfield, had been attacked by a phantom hair-snipper who vanished soon afterwards. A certain bus route through Orpington was also put on alert when several young women reported having their hair cut by an unseen individual.

Even stranger is a peculiar section of text extracted from *The beauties of England and Wales; or Delineations of each county* by a John Britton, who records:

Strange news from Arpington near Bexley in Kent; being a true narrative of a young Maid who was possest with several Devils, or Evil Spirits, one of which, by the Prayers of the pious and religious

Doctor, who came to visit her, was fetcht out of her Body, and appeared in the Room, in the Likeness of a large Snake, and twisted itself about the Doctor's Neck, whilst he was at his Devotion. With an Account also of other Devils, which yet remain in her, and reveal strange Things; the like never heard of before, of which the Contents within will give you a particular Account. The narrative is attested by several Persons of Credit; but amongst many others, by one Mrs Hopper, a Person of Worth, and good Reputation, whom you may speak with at the Sign of the Bell and Draggon, in White's-Ally, in Chancery-Lane, who was there present whilst this Accident happened.

There are several reputedly haunted buildings in Orpington including Downe Court. The building was constructed in the seventeenth century. It is said to be the haunt of a young girl who, with soaking wet appearance, is known to appear at the bedside of those sleeping in a certain room. She often makes her presence known by a terrible sobbing noise. She is in distress because she drowned many years ago in the old moat and seems to forever loiter in miserable limbo. The phantom girl is not alone however. Downe Court has several other resident spooks. One being that of an old man who was said to have often been seen in the barn. Author Andrew Green investigated a number of hauntings in this house and spoke of a severed arm that apparently startled a young woman who was sleeping in one of the bedrooms. The phantom limb allegedly had appeared on the bed beside her. A couple of rooms in the house were said to have been so haunted that exorcisms were performed to rid them of their evil atmosphere. According to legend, a former owner named Brian Thompson, who purchased Downe Court in 1962, took a photo which was said to contain several ghosts. Author Peter Underwood when analysing the photograph was quick to remark that, 'I can't see one that could not be the result of an unusual combination of light and shade!'

Even so, in 1962 Downe Court, when purchased by Mr Thompson, was rather run down. His aim was to restore the property to its former glory but due to the persistent strange atmospheres, the manor never flourished. Andrew Green mentioned numerous encounters told to him by witnesses. One included a sighting of just the head and shoulders of a spectral cavalier. Other witnesses had reported hearing the sound of fighting in one of the rooms whilst other visitors mentioned a certain spot on the stairway where an overwhelming feeling of dread would ensue. Coincidentally this is said to be the exact spot where many years ago a group of cavaliers hanged a man. Other rumours claim that the house may have once been used for black magic rituals, and that the negative spirits remain dormant until triggered by an unsuspecting visitor. In his book *Our Haunted Kingdom*, Green adds that Mr Thompson told him, 'We've been fighting a family curse there …'

Downe Court appears to have caused some confusion among supernatural authors. Andrew Green states that Charles Darwin wrote his 'world-shattering book *The Origin of the Species*' in the grounds but writer Antony D. Hippisley Coxe, whilst writing of the haunting, was quick to mention that one must 'not mistake this place for Downe House which lies across the road from one entrance to the

Downe House – does naturalist Charles Darwin still haunt this building?

Court, and which was Darwin's home and is now his museum.' Interestingly the grounds of Darwin's former home are said to be haunted. Could it be that the spectre of the naturalist still frequents his old haunt? In 2003 a lady named Philippa Coulthard began working in the grounds of Downe House as a trainee gardener. The man she'd replaced had told her that should she see an elderly man, with a long white beard, sporting a black cape, not to be alarmed, as he was simply an eccentric who liked to wander the village. The man had been seen in the grounds of the house, often strolling on foggy, dew-damp mornings along a section of pathway known as Sand Walk. This had been the same pathway that Charles Darwin was said to have strolled all those years ago.

Philippa was so intrigued by the mention of the bearded gentleman that she made enquiries in the village only to be told there was no such man. Is it possible that the figure seen on Darwin's 'thinking path' was in fact the naturalist, albeit in ghostly form?

Downe has several other ghostly tales of note. One comes from a Lucy M. Gonin who resided at Shortlands. She once spoke of owning a photograph taken of her by a friend at a field in Downe. The photo, according to Lucy, was said to show the ghostly figure of a man wearing a

A haunted building which sat on Rookery Road was once rumoured to have three resident ghosts.

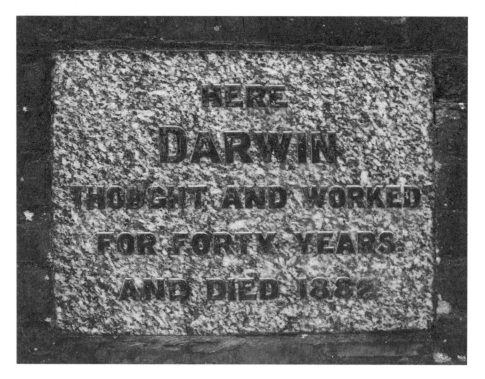

Plaque on the wall outside Downe House.

three-pointed crown upon his head. Lucy also mentions how, 'A second face apparently half submerged in water appears in the same snapshot.'

A house known as the Rookery, situated on Rookery Road in Downe also has a ghost story attached to it. A former resident of the building was a Mrs Mary Knox Johnston. One night she was awoken by the sound of a fight taking place in the hall. She scrambled to her feet but upon investigation found no sign of a disturbance. A few nights later the sound of breaking glass was heard, but again a search found nothing. A lady who used to live in the area once told Mary that the house had always been haunted and that those who lived there didn't stay long. The local legend claimed that a spectral cavalier and two ghostly young boys were said to haunt the building.

Another haunted site of note is Kevington Hall. Located on the Crockenhill Road, Kevington Hall was built in the late 1760s. Whilst the hall may not be haunted, its grounds could well be. Author John Love told me that during the Second World War a German plane crashed into the nearby woods and the pilot was killed. There have been occasional reports of a shadowy figure lurking in the woodland, but whether it's the spectre of the pilot we'll never know. Some witnesses have described a sudden drop in temperature, and feeling nauseous. Kevington itself sits just a mile south-east of St Mary Cray. This rural hamlet also goes by the name Kevingtown. The name derives from the Old English 'place on a small hill.'

There used to be a legend of a reputedly haunted house in Orpington, said to sit on what used to be called Dalton Way. In the 1960s there was rumour that a builder died after a terrible accident in one of the houses, and his ghost was believed to loiter in the building, but no further light can be shed on this tale. A building known as Borkwood House – an Edwardian build – was said to be haunted. The ghost is mentioned in a letter I found in Bromley library and comes from a lady named Mrs Eileen Saunders who, in 1975 lived on Lancing Road, Orpington. In her letter she wrote of meeting a lady who used to work at Borkwood House as a cook. The building eventually became a school. The cook spoke openly about the ghosts to Mrs Saunders, stating that her room was in the top attic and that 'many a time the ghosts arrived,' usually in the form of 'a carriage containing a lady, covered with glittering diamonds' who was accompanied by a smartly dressed gentleman. Several witnesses had reported hearing the sound of the carriage as it approached the house but upon getting close to the door the sound would fade.

In her letter Mrs Saunders also briefly mentions hauntings at buildings known as the Limes and Barn Awe but doesn't go into detail about the ghosts. Meanwhile, the Artichoke pub, which used to sit in the High Street of Orpington, was reputedly haunted in the mid-1990s by an old lady. The building is now home to a Turkish restaurant.

Fordcroft phantoms

According to the *Ancient Monuments* website, 'Several excavations have been carried out at a possible Roman villa and Early Medieval cemetery site at Bellefield Road, Poverest and Fordcroft Road.' The *Bromley Times* reported that, Cray Avenue, which runs close to Bellefield Road and Poverest Road, '… is one of the oldest sites along the Cray Valley, being the site of an ancient Roman bath house.'

The newspaper added that several artefacts were discovered in the area during the construction of cottages at Fordcroft. Strangely, ever since such premises were built on the site, ghost stories have done the rounds. One family seemed to be the centre of such paranormal activity. A Hetty Dunmall, who resided at one of the cottages, remarked that when her grandmother came to stay with her family in the 1980s, lots of odd things began to happen. She told *The Times* in 1982 that, 'Granny had a four-poster bed with brass rails around and heavy red brocade curtains. Each morning we would find the curtains twisted round and round, which granny could not have possibly managed to do herself.'

On another occasion when Hetty's granny awoke, an old oak table had been flipped over. This coincided with a sighting of a ghostly man which seemed to unnerve Hetty's grandmother to the extent that the entire family decided to keep watch one night. Hetty added, 'My husband checked at 2 a.m. and everything was alright so we decided to get to sleep. In the morning the curtains were twisted round the rail, the table overturned and a piece of cast iron fender had been broken off and stuffed behind the old gas stove.'

The cottages at Fordcroft were eventually knocked down but archaeologists excavating the site made a staggering discovery. According to the newspaper, beneath the soil, where Hetty's grandmothers' ground floor bedroom once sat, the skeleton of a Roman soldier was unearthed. However, Marie-Louise Kerr, curator at Bromley Museum, and who I am indebted to for the information, concluded, 'Any ghostly soldiers would have been Anglo-Saxons rather than the Romans, if anything at all! The Anglo-Saxon burials were found with swords, spears and shield bosses. I don't imagine any Romans went to their Bath House in full armour!'

Supernatural at St Paul's Cray

St Paul's Cray, of the Bromley district, was once described as being on 'the rivulet Cray'. Although now incorporated into Orpington, like its sister St Mary Cray, it once existed as a separate entity. The more wooded parts of the area melt into the grounds of Scadbury Park, mentioned elsewhere. In the sixteenth century the area was recorded as Paul Crey.

Researchers John and Anne Spencer have spent many years investigating ghosts. In their book *The Encyclopaedia of Ghosts & Spirits* they feature an intriguing tale from Orpington. They interviewed a fellow named Mr D. Park, of St Paul's Cray who told them that on a summers day in 1982 he'd been standing in the bedroom belonging to his grandmother, staring out the window, when something appeared out of the corner of his eye reflected in the mirror. Mr Park turned and was confronted by a figure adorned in black. The apparition wasn't fully visible as it had reclined into the shadows of the corner of the room, but to Mr Park the spectre resembled a monk. John and Anne Spencer were told of another

spooky encounter, again involving a mirror only this time involving Mr Park's mother. She'd been given a 3ft-tall antique mirror as a wedding gift. She put the mirror in her bedroom but one day, whilst moving the mirror to another room in the house, noticed in the reflection a figure that appeared indistinct and in the distance. So unnerved was she by this sighting that she stored the mirror away in a cupboard, condemning it as evil. According to Mr Park his mother seemed to be plagued with misfortune, and always blamed the mirror, until one day she decided to break the cursed object and threw it in the shed. However, although Mr Park often felt a strong air of dread whenever he saw the mirror, his mother's quality of living improved once the mirror was cast away.

Ghostly grandfather

Mr D. Park also told John and Anne Spencer that he was brought up by his grandparents, but in 1982 his grandfather died. After his loss, Mr Park reported a number of strange things that began to occur in the house. Mr Park was thirteen when his grandfather passed, and one day whilst in the front part of the house he heard his grandfather call his name. Looking back years later, Mr Park put this down to the fact that he had been grieving severely and maybe his mind was playing tricks, however, his grandmother also mentioned something peculiar. She told him that the night after their loss; she had got into bed when she suddenly felt the presence of her husband next to her. From then on there would be sudden drops in temperature, the sound of footsteps throughout the house – often heard to enter his grandmother's room. Another eerie factor to the haunting emerged when Mr Park was told by his grandmother that the house had been built in the 1950s on the site of an old orchard. Centuries previous to this a monastery sat on the site.

Mr Park never found out whether it was his grandfather, or someone else haunting the house, although he did recall how when his grandfather was ill, items throughout the house would move of their own accord. Only when his grandfather passed did the activity cease.

A frightened family

In 1982 a family of three were driven out of their St Paul's Cray home by a ghost. A Mrs Christine Robinson and her two children vowed never to return to their house at Breakspears Drive after six months of what they described as hell in the hands of a seemingly mischievous spirit. The ghost was blamed for turning electrical appliances on and off, the sudden icy cold temperatures, a strong stench of burning, and also turning taps on and off. The two children, one barely into his teens and the other aged twelve, often saw the apparition – a misty figure with blonde hair and wearing a white shirt. The children also reported seeing the ghost of a small boy who also appeared to a child belonging to a former tenant. The ghost, rather eerily, spoke to the little girl and told her his name was Peter and ordered her to go away with him. The little girl fled in terror but shortly afterwards was struck down with meningitis.

Mrs Robinson told the *Orpington Times* of 20 May 1982, 'I gradually became more bad tempered when I was living there. I would be rude to people, and try to never see my relatives.'

Although Mrs Robinson's son Julian had experienced the paranormal activity, the family believed that the spirits were most likely to affect women, young and old. She added, 'I just don't know what to do next. I am waiting to hear from the council what they are going to do. I would not exchange with anyone else … it wouldn't be fair.'

The following week the newspaper carried the headline, 'Haunted house claims "rubbish"' in response to a former tenant of the property, named Joyce Ellinor, who came forward to report that she'd never experienced anything whilst living at the house. When asked about her own daughters experience with a 'ghost' she responded, '"My girl had an imaginary friend like lots of little children … that's all it was".'

Even so, after the story broke, a neighbour of Mrs Robinson claimed she was 'fed up' of people gathering outside the reputedly haunted house in search of ghosts. She told *The Times*, 'We've had so many kids around here and I've had to call the police up here twice.'

On 3 June the newspaper gave one last word on the alleged haunting, stating that a psychic investigator had visited the property and found nothing. Investigator Bob Cracknell told the paper, 'Frankly, I was wasting my time,' after coming away with no evidence the building was ghost infested. He concluded, 'I have asked Mrs Robinson to come back to the house with me. She may be a catalyst that starts it off.'

6

EERIE BICKLEY

The residential area of Bickley has a population of almost 14,000 people. It can be found between the areas of Bromley, Chislehurst, Petts Wood and Sundgridge Park. In his work *Imperial Gazetteer of England and Wales*, John Maruis Wilson describes Bickley as 'a chapelry with a railway station, in Bromley parish,

The Chequers pub at Bickley has a long-standing ghost story attached to it.

Kent, 1½ mile E of Bromley, Pop., 473.' The name Bickley is said to derive from 'Bicca's clearing,' and was uninhabited as a place up until the eighteenth century.

Nowhere chillier than The Chequers

There is nothing cosier than a haunted pub on a crisp winter evening. Customers snuggled around a crackling log fire, clasping a jug of ale or glass of spirit in frost-bitten hands. They huddle safe and warm from the biting winds and stare out of the frost-laced windows. Ghost stories are often best suited to autumnal evenings or more so during the festive season. In Bickley there is a pub with a very haunted history. The Chequers pub, situated on Southborough Lane, could well be one of the most haunted pubs in England. The pub dates back to the 1500s and in the past distinguished guests such as Samuel Pepys, the naval administrator and MP, as well as author Charles Dickens, visited the pub. On 29 October 2008 the *Bromley Times* ran a feature for Halloween concerning the alleged ghosts of the old inn. The report, featured under the heading, 'Spirits alive at Dick Turpin's old haunt?' spoke of a gaggle of ghouls said to lurk in the pubs darkest corners. 'A French policeman, a woman in stiletto heels and a poltergeist that forces visitors against walls', being just a trio of the terrors that the newspaper named. The report quoted pub managers – husband and wife team Danny and Sarah Goldsborough – who claimed to have had several peculiar experiences in the pub.

'When I first took over the pub,' commented Danny, 'I heard the footsteps of a female in high heels. I looked over my shoulder but there was nothing there.' On another occasion Danny claimed that his two-year-old little girl had been 'talking' to an invisible presence.

The most famous spectre said to inhabit the pub is that of Dick Turpin. Or so the legend claims. In his book *Ghosts of Kent*, author Peter Underwood mentions how in life the notorious highwayman 'often visited this place, using the back stairs when necessary to make a hasty disappearance.' A few decades ago a barmaid reported having an encounter with a man dressed in green velvet and confirmed this had been the ghost of Turpin. Underwood also records how a visitor had a similar experience whilst peeking into one of the rooms. A man dressed in green and 'wearing a hat with a plume in it' was seen to be sitting at a table and writing with a quill pen. A search of the room proved fruitless as there was no sign of the mysterious man. To corroborate the more recent stories of phantom footfalls, a previous landlord mentioned how he'd heard footsteps on numerous occasions along with the sound of slamming doors. Any time these noises would be investigated, there would be no sign of any intruder and in most cases the doors were locked shut. The footsteps would often be heard as if emanating from one of the older rooms in the upper part of the pub. On several occasions the slamming doors and eerie footsteps seemed to work in cohorts, with the footfalls being heard then immediately followed by the banging of a door. The same landlord had an even more unnerving experience one night when he was awoken by the shaking of his bed. However, when he leapt to his feet there was no sign of anyone else in the room.

The ghost story seemed to come to light in the late 1960s when the pub was owned by a Mr Gordon and his wife, Eileen. They took over the pub during the late 1950s, the first bouts of activity seemingly focused on a case of gin which on three occasions had been moved by unseen hands. On other occasions the case would be toppled over, leaving a handful of bottles broken.

Although the Turpin-related ghost story has embedded itself into the fabric of the building and the local community, it would seem that Dick Turpin, after death, is one of the most travelled of lost souls. More than sixty locations across Britain are said to be haunted by Turpin's spectre, suggesting that this ghost is constantly on the move or that the locals are keen to blame any vague bout of paranormal activity on the infamous highwayman.

The female ghosts of the public house could well be echoes from the eighteenth century. They were said to haunt the upper part of the house although Mr Gordon never had any encounters with such spirits.

The creepiest experience involving Mr Gordon took place one night when he was awoken by the shaking of his bed. Strangely, Eileen wasn't disturbed by the tumult. However, on a few

Is the Chequers pub haunted by a ghostly highwayman, thought to be the notorious Dick Turpin? (Illustration by E. Rodrigo)

occasions when Mr Gordon had gone on holiday – leaving his wife at home – friends who stayed to help her out also reported the terrible sleepless nights and the violent shaking of their beds. Mr Gordon commented that, 'These strange things only seem to affect some people. I suppose some of us are psychic and others are not. But I think there is something in this house – if there is such thing as a ghost, I think there is one here.'

7

PECULIAR PENGE

The suburb of Penge is situated in the London Borough of Bromley. In the year 957 the area is noted as a small town called Penceat – the name possibly deriving from the Celtic word meaning 'edge of the wood', as the surrounding areas used to harbour rich woodlands.

Penge pub spooks

Penge has a haunted pub or two. The Hollywood East public house used to be known as the Park Tavern and sits on Station Road. In the winter of 2012 I was contacted by a Penge resident who had a few stories to tell. He commented:

> In the 1800s the pub used to house the coroner's office and the mortuary used to be in the cellar. I used to drink there in the 1970s up until 1990 and it was common knowledge between staff and customers that the pub was haunted. No one knew exactly what haunted the building but when there used to be a few late night lock-in's there were often

times when glasses would fly off the shelf and never smash despite hitting a wall or the floor. Certain items would be moved around the place, pictures on the wall would move of their own accord and there were certain spots that were absolutely freezing cold. You expect some areas of a pub to be cold, but this was far too cold. People would report being touched by an invisible presence and some staff and customers would often talk about being watched or followed by something unseen. Some people believe that the ghostly activity used to take place when somebody in the building was doing something wrong, suggesting that the ghosts were unhappy.

Another reputedly haunted pub in the town is the Pawleyne Arms, also known as the Pauline Arms. The pub can be found at No. 156, High Street opposite the railway station. Rumour has it that many years ago there was a grisly murder of a girl in the vicinity and it is believed that her spectre still roams the pub in its forlorn state.

The unseen chicken killer and the phantom cat-ripper!

For a number of years there have been reports throughout the Bromley of what people like to call 'big cats' on the loose. These elusive creatures are said to resemble 'panthers' (melanistic leopards) and pumas. Despite the fact evidence to support these creatures seems scarce, the eyewitness reports continue. Theories put forward to explain these mysterious animals maintain that they are offspring of animals released in the 1970s, when it was relatively common for people to keep exotic cats as pets. Many of these were released into the wilds after the introduction of the Dangerous Wild Animals Act in 1976, which forced owners to pay for a licence. The large cats seen around the borough have been dubbed names such as 'the beast of Bromley' or the 'Penge puma' and such animals have embedded themselves into local folklore. Other theories put forward to explain such beasts are that they are nothing more than large domestic cats or misidentifications of dogs and foxes. More diverse theories suggest such animals are of a ghostly nature, whilst more down-to-earth explanations are that these cats are escapees from zoo parks or private collections. Either way, the debate rages and it is a fascinating subject. However, such animals have been blamed for several grisly animal killings over the last decade particularly in the Bromley area. In 2012 there was a spate of chicken decapitations in Penge. Fourteen beheaded birds were found in the Avington Grove area. The bodies were completely bereft of blood leading some people to think that some type of vampyric ghoul was roaming the night. However, an American researcher named Rick Ross, based in New Jersey, was of the opinion that the macabre decapitations may have been the result of some ritual sacrifice as the heads were missing.

This wasn't the first time that Penge and the nearby suburbs had to cope with such decapitations. In 1998 several domestic cats were found dead across the borough, their heads had been removed and blood drained. Newspapers at the time called the elusive assailant the 'phantom cat-ripper' and the RSPCA were bombarded with calls from worried pet owners. Strangely the authorities pinned the blame on vehicles despite the fact that the decapitated cats were found in back gardens and away from roads. The killings continued right through to 2001 when the head of a white domestic cat was found in a Penge back garden. Animal expert Trevor Smith examined some of the carcasses and concluded that, 'These killings are not the work of a fox. In some cases the animal's rib cage has been chewed off. It is very possible that this is the work of a big cat.'

No-one is sure what exactly killed those chickens or domestic cats, but a Mrs Smith who once resided in Penge claimed that one night she had seen a small shadowy figure in her back garden and blamed this phantom intruder for the death of her cat. The woman, who found her decapitated pet the next morning, told me in 2001, 'The carcass of my beloved cat was drained of blood and bereft of a head. What scared me most is that the kill resembled those drained carcasses found on the island of Puerto Rico and which were attributed to a phantasmal creature known as the chupacabra which translates as "goat sucker".'

During the hysteria a criminal profiler was sent in to analyse the case and claimed that some type of domestic cat serial killer was on the loose but whatever killed those cats is still out there, stalking the neighbourhood like the ghost some people still believe it to be.

8

WEST WICKHAM WEIRDNESS

The town of West Wickham is said to be situated on an old Roman Road. The area is first recorded as far back as the eleventh century, although the name dates back several centuries previous, deriving from the Roman word 'vicus'.

A gaggle of ghosts

When one considers the amount of traffic accidents that have taken place on some of Britain's roads, it's no wonder that people, on occasion, report ghosts on quiet lanes and busy roads

A friend of mine named Paul Masters, a long-time resident of West Wickham, spoke to me recently regarding several local ghost stories. He lives at Coney Hall which is a suburban district that was built in the 1930s. He stated:

> There is a story told by the locals that the local church (St John's) off of Coney Hall recreation ground is haunted. A former girlfriend of mine said her mum saw what appeared to be a ghostly

figure of a woman close to the outer perimeter wall near the roadside. This took place in the 1980s. She'd been walking home from a night out when the incident occurred. Many locals have also added that the nearby school (West Wickham Court School) has had fairly frequent sightings of a ghost, especially around the area of the car-park. Teenagers hanging around the area in the past have reported a few vague apparitions including the spectre of a woman. It's worth noting that Wickham Court has a similar build structure to St James Palace built by Henry Haydon in 1469 and whose great niece was Anne Boleyn, who it is said was courted by Henry VIII while staying there. The rumour I've heard is that she spent either her last few hours there before her death there and it is in fact her spirit said to be seen roaming the vicinity.

In his work *Highways & Byways of Kent*, Walter Jerrold comments on Wickham Court as a 'handsome Tudor manor house' and, in regards to the Anne

A woman in white has been seen near St John's Church in West Wickham.

Boleyn association, that 'Anne stayed at the house during some part of the time that the King was planning to clear her way to the throne.' Her ghost is also said to roam a part of the grounds known as Anne Boleyn's Walk. The main problem with this ghost story, however, is the rumour that the spectre of Anne is said to haunt so many locations across the country. I'm unsure if ghosts have boundaries, but certain famous spirits seem to pop up in so many locations.

Paul Masters also went on to speak of a few more local spook tales:

At the junction of Croydon Road and Kingsway, where Wickes store now stands, just to the left if you're facing it, is a fenced off small lake or reservoir. Back in the 1950s the area was open and kids often used to visit it. A group of young boys were playing football there and their ball went into the water. One of the lads went to recover the ball and got snagged by some dumped waste and drowned. Ever since this tragic accident a faint childish cry has been heard as if calling for help. People coming out of one of the local pubs during the early hours have heard these cries and on another occasion a man claimed to have seen a boy floundering in the water. The witness rushed to the aid of the youth but when he reached the location there was no sign of the drowning boy. It's since been fenced off and was drained back in the '80s but nothing odd was reported. It's still full with water today because of an underground spring.

Paul added,

The A2022 Kent gateway, known as the Mad Mile is the local 'boy racers' haunt!

West Wickham Court School peeps out eerily from behind the trees.

I've known of at least two deaths in the last twelve years on that road, one concerning a police officer who was hit around five years ago by two cars which were racing. Another story that does the rounds tells of a thirty-year-old man

The roads between West Wickham, Hayes and Biggin Hill are said to be frequented by spirits.

who was driving a sports car during an icy January sometime during the 1980s. He'd been travelling too fast and hit a patch of black ice; he lost control of the vehicle. Whilst growing up I actually heard the stories of the 'phantom car' being seen on foggy winter's nights. The ghost car would be seen swerving and crashing at a distance only to make no sound or leave no trace.

To round off his batch of ghostly yarns Paul told me of another road-related spectre. 'The mother of my son told me that her friend's dad was a minicab driver and had once observed a ghostly child whilst he'd been pulled up to take a break in the clearing of Preston Road. At first he began to get a feeling as if he wasn't alone in the area and then saw the ghost.'

According to Paul other taxi drivers had also reported the same eerie feelings.

A spook at The Swan

On 26 November 1981 the *Beckenham & Penge Advertiser* reported 'Ghostly goings on greet new couple' after pub owners George and Toni Herberts had taken over the Swan in West Wickham High Street. It was said that the resident ghost, named Geoffrey, had been up to his old tricks, keeping the new landlords up with a series of loud bangs, thuds and phantom footsteps. According to the newspaper, Toni had been awoken by strange noises and a door that opened of its own accord. She told the paper, 'I'm convinced it was him but I wasn't frightened – he's quite a friendly chap and I don't think he would harm anyone.'

Geoffrey is said to be the ghost of a former landlord who hanged himself.

A ghost at The Grove

During the late 1960s and early '70s a family at the Grove, in West Wickham were pestered by a pesky spook that had to eventually be driven out of their home. Canon John Pearce-Higgins of Southwark Cathedral, accompanied by two spiritual mediums, was called in by the unnamed family in 1971 after items, such as kitchen utensils, had begun to disappear. Doors were reported as opening and then slamming of their own accord and the family dog would spend a lot of its time barking at an unseen intruder. On one occasion the garden gate opened and clicked shut as if someone had walked up the path towards the house. Canon Pearce-Higgins exorcised the house and a psychic medium claimed that the resident entity was that of an elderly woman who died in the house.

The Swan in West Wickham.

9

ST MARY CRAY STRANGENESS

St Mary Cray is situated on the River Cray within the London Borough of Bromley. Centuries ago the town was known as South Cray although historian Edward Hasted records '… but so early as King Edward I's reign it was known by its present name.'

A ghostly man and more

The White Swan public house (now a Chinese takeaway) is said to date back to the mid part of the nineteenth century. A former owner named Norman Pointer recalled being hit on the back by a pewter mug, an act which he couldn't account for. Some blame a poltergeist within the pub for the unusual activity which usually involves glasses moving and falling of their own accord. Some who've experienced the poltergeist have given it a pet name, Jack, although no one seems to have actually seen the resident spirit. Fleeting shadows out of the corner of the eye seem to be the usual thing, although Mr Pointer stated quite categorically that on one occasion a relative of his 'clearly' saw a figure 'walking through the bottom bar.' Could this mystery spectre be the spirit of an elderly man who hanged himself in the dank cellar in the early 1900s? Who knows?

The Mary Rose restaurant, now a hotel, sits on the High Street in St Mary Cray. It was once rumoured to have been haunted. A few decades ago the then joint landlady reported that one evening a young lady had knocked at the door of the inn. She had become lost after attempting to deliver a parcel and so she was asked into the building. She asked the second chef if she could take a look round and when they reached a room with a four-poster bed in it she exclaimed, 'There's a ghost here!'

It turns out that the woman with the parcel was also a medium and she claimed that the resident spectre was a female who had been very happy in the building. The pub was believed to have been built on the site of a fourteenth-century chapel and numerous odd things had taken place over the course of a few years.

Another owner stated that in the past the piano in one of the rooms had started playing as if someone was sitting there tinkling the ivories. On another occasion doors left open had been found locked and there had been numerous freezing cold spots experienced in the building.

There is a brief mention of the inn being haunted by a spectral lady with 'coal black eyes' on the website Edith's Streets. The blog, which includes a post devoted to the 'Thames Tributary – Cray flowing to Darent, St Paul's Cray' also mentions the haunted property the Mary Rose, at No. 40-50 in the High Street, and now converted to a restaurant.

The Mary Rose phantom was still active up until 1984 and reported in the *Orpington Times* of 3 May 1984 under the heading: 'Ghost saga: New twist'. They mentioned that restaurant owner Michael Chaston had observed the ghost of a woman wearing a long white dress and having long black hair. Michael had been at the back of the bar after midnight when the wraith appeared from the side of the fireplace and drifted across the room before disappearing.

A haunted house in St Mary Cray is mentioned in the *Orpington Times* of 12 May 1983 under the heading: 'Terrified family flee house of ghosts.' The story, written by reporter Anne Blythe concerned a house on Star Lane and the King family who claimed to have been driven out of their home by things that went bump in the night. Martin King, the owner, told the newspaper that he'd seen a strange ghostly face that had appeared in front of him

one night. He shared his encounter with his mother-in-law who stated that she'd seen the same entity.

Martin's wife was next to experience something terrifying. One evening she felt something tug at her leg and was suddenly thrown down the stairs. Then there were the mornings when the couple would wake to find all the photographs of the children turned face down. Mr King told the newspaper, 'We would be sitting, watching television, and hear footsteps upstairs. One night I walked past my daughter's bedroom and saw a figure standing over her bed.'

Mr King was so disturbed by what he'd seen that he decided to move his family downstairs so they could all be together when they slept. The paranormal activity had become so distressing that Mr King decided to call in Revd Ralph Osborne to bless the house. However, after Mr Osborne left, Mr King was confronted once again with the ghastly face and with that bundled his family into their car and drove them to his mother-in-law's. He then returned with his mother-in law and stayed, telling the newspaper, 'I am too frightened to leave the house; I don't want to lose it. We have worked hard to make it look nice but I think this ghost is malicious and I am worried about my family.'

Mr King's fears were corroborated by neighbour Jean Townsend who commented that she'd lived next to the house for almost twenty years and heard about the resident ghost. She said, 'At least three previous tenants have said the house was haunted.'

10

LEGENDS OF PRATT'S BOTTOM

The *Pratts Bottom Community* Website states that the village, which lies on the border with Kent 'nestles in the Green Belt, on the dip slope of the North Downs, and oozes with history.' In a 1773 record the village is mentioned as Spratts Bottom but more likely changed due to the inhabitancy of the Pratt family.

The Bull's Head at Pratt's Bottom. Is this pub another haunt of highwayman Dick Turpin?

To be taken with a pinch of salt

A majority of the fleeting ghosts observed in the village could well be those of smugglers. This would be no surprise when one considers that just a few centuries ago smugglers and highwaymen would frequent some of the dark hollows and misty corners of the village. Smugglers were often said to create ghostly tales for certain areas in order to keep people from uncovering the contraband they'd stashed somewhere. The notorious Dick Turpin was said to hide up in a local public house called the Bull's Head. According to the pub website, Turpin often visited '… before being caught horse stealing in 1739 and hanged for his crime.'

In his time it seems as if Turpin visited a large number of pubs, which seems unlikely considering how difficult the notorious highwayman was to catch. The already mentioned Chequers at Bickley was said to be another of his haunts, so every time a shadowy figure is seen in one of these public houses, you can be sure that the spirit of Turpin will be blamed.

One alleged Pratts Bottom ghost story was mentioned in magazine *Loaded*, of all places, under the heading: 'I fell for Jasper; the really friendly ghost.' However, such a spoof story was most certainly taken with a huge pinch of salt, despite its claim that it was submitted by twenty-seven-year-old Pratts Bottom resident Sally Lowe. The story was written very much tongue-in-cheek, possibly due to the unusual nature of the village name which the magazine decided to poke fun at.

11

HORROR AT HAYES

The town of Hayes was recorded in the twelfth century as Hoese, meaning 'a settlement in open land overgrown with shrubs and rough bushes.'

The haunting horse of Hayes

There is an obscure ghost story from Hayes mentioned fleetingly in the *Nottingham Evening Post* of 28 May 1926. The brief article states that 'A meadow at Hayes, Kent, in which there is a 12 foot high memorial to a horse, is said to be haunted by a phantom horseman.' The article adds that, 'The memorial was erected by the late Mr Goodhart of Beckenham to his favourite riding horse, buried underneath …' According to the source the ghost is said to be that of Mr Goodhart, mounted upon his white horse. Several witnesses at the time reported that the spectre was seen to glide across the meadow of a misty night and pass the memorial before vanishing as it reached the hedge that bordered the golf course at Park Langley.

The white lady of Hayes Common

In 2012 I was contacted by a man named Richard. He told me a very spooky story which was related to him by his late father, Peter, who, whilst travelling home late one night in 1947, and accompanied by his friend Stan, had had a strange experience involving a white lady. In his letter to me, Richard wrote:

> Here is all the information I have gathered from Stan Howe about the White Lady of Hayes Common. In 1947 my late father Peter Thompson, aged eighteen at the time, and his friend Stan Howe, twenty, were driving (Stan was driving) home after a night out in Stan's Morris 6 along the A232 Croydon Road travelling towards West Wickham. As they approached the junction with Hartfield Crescent the headlights of the car illuminated a white spectral figure of a woman with indistinct features and dressed in a long flowing dress.

Five Elms Road in Hayes. Said to be the haunt of a ghostly man. This photo shows a mysterious ghostly orb – which sadly turned out to be nothing more than moisture in the air!

She was seen by both men and was perceived to be travelling from right to left and clearly floating above the road surface. Stan was so interested in what he saw that he did some research and uncovered that something bad had taken place in some cottages further up the road towards Farnborough. Interestingly, a girl that I know named Carol was in a car with her father driving at night along Five Elms Road, when a white figure of a man appeared in front of him. He drove straight through the figure. This must've been about 1981.

Richard was accustomed to paranormal activity, he continued, 'A few years ago now, in the October of 1990 I was driving up a lane in my Ford Sierra – it was late – when I noticed a strange glowing ball of light, roughly the size of a basketball, that drifted high above a hedge and moved out of sight. At the time I recall looking at my dashboard to check if there was any light from within that may have reflected somewhere but there wasn't. This floating light was cobalt blue in colour but the most unnerving thing about it was that during the experience I felt very unwell. Then, around ten years later when I was working for a local taxi company I picked up an elderly lady and we got talking about ghosts and she happened to mention that in the same road there had been rumour of a spectral male figure said to be seen running up and down the lane.'

12

SCARY SUNDRIDGE

Sundridge can be found in the northern part of the Bromley borough.

The haunted manor

In the work *Outlines of the History and Antiquities of Bromley, in Kent*, John Dunkin speaks of a 'Manor in Sundridge' stating that it sits 'towards the north-east corner of this parish, among the woods …' and that it was once owned by the distinguished Blands family. Sundridge Park Manor today is, according to the manor website, 'one of the region's most elegant luxury hotels,' and also a premier wedding venue. The building is a Grade I listed manor house designed in the 1700s. Dunkin quotes chronicler Edward Hasted in regards to the reputed spectre of the building, 'This time-stricken mansion offers a favourable opportunity for any daring ghost to play his vagaries; and it does not seem to be neglected: for I was solemnly assured that noises had been often heard in and about the house, sometimes as if the furniture fell down and broke to pieces, and that once a lady appeared dressed in white, with a lighted torch in her hand, accompanied by a gentleman in dark clothes, with a high-crowned broad-brimmed hat which flapped over the sides of his face!!!' Strangely this ghost story seems to bear great similarity to that of Simpson's Place mentioned earlier in the book.

A short distance from Sundridge Park you'll find Crescent Road. In the *Bromley Times* of 6 November 1964 there is brief mention of a spectre at this location. Peggy Martyn Clark stated, 'It appears that in 1878 there was a great flood in Bromley, so severe that a lake 40ft long formed in Crescent Road, much to the consternation of all around. Maybe this [the ghost] is some woman looking for a loved one or thing which she lost in those terrifying waters. Who can say?'

13

UNCANNY CHELSFIELD

The small village of Chelsfield is recorded from the eleventh century as Cillesfelle, the word is said to derive from the meaning 'land of a man called Cêol', although historian Edward Hasted states that the name Chelsfield originated from its 'cold and open situation.' In Saxon the word ceald or cile is said to mean cold with feld meaning field. Although Hasted writes of Chelsfield as 'having nothing remarkable in it' there are a handful of ghostly tales to speak of. Chelsfield has a smuggling history too. A network of tunnels and caves were said to wind beneath the village, these dark corners no doubt acted as ideal hiding places for local criminals.

Screaming Angie and a ghost that followed someone home

A few years ago now a former Chelsfield resident decided to revisit his childhood haunts. Accompanied by a friend he drove to Kent from an unnamed location and settled in the public house known as the Bo Peep. This pub, situated on Hewitts Road in the village, began life as a farm building constructed during the reign of King Edward VI (1537-1553). Over the years the inn has had a couple of other names, including Seagraves and the White Hart. The name Bo Peep could well derive from a smuggling rhyme – Bo Peep was the name of a small cove near Hastings. When the pub was known as the White Hart there was rumour that a tunnel used by smugglers used to wind its way beneath the building and finish at a disused well in Crockenhill. According to the pub website, 'The White Hart often came under the scrutiny of Customs' Riding Officers' and in 1783 the inn was mentioned in a statement made by one John Kelly, a Riding Officer, to his superiors at Hastings. It reads:

We are in possession of sufficient facts to know that smugglers are taking every method to improve their trading and also conveying immense quantities of spirits to London. They have warehouses at proper distances on the roads. One such place of hiding is a dense wooded area near Orpington called 'Bo Peep'. My men and I have been watchful of a drinking house there called The White Hart.

The Bo Peep is the kind of pub you'd expect to have a ghostly tale, and it doesn't disappoint. The resident spectre is known as Screaming Angie, thought to be the spirit of a girl aged around six or seven, who many years ago was put into the cellar by her uncle after receiving a telling off. The story goes that, albeit rather bizarrely, the little girl was forgotten all about and eventually died in the room. The cellar, now disused, runs under the dining area of the pub. This room used to be a skittle alley.

The ghost at the Bo Peep is known as Screaming Angie. (Illustration by E. Rodrigo)

The Bo Peep public house in Chelsfield.

In January 2013 a member of staff told me that the little girl ghost is said to wear a white dress. When I questioned as to why she is known as Screaming Angie, I was told that on certain nights the occasional strange screaming noise can be heard echoing through certain parts of the building. Is the noise merely the wind or the ghostly girl, still trying to escape the confines of the cellar?

There is a possibility that the chap who visited the pub with his friend may have taken one of the resident spirits home with him! The unnamed witness used to live in a house next door to the pub. It had been a frosty December when the two friends chatted in the pub about old times, but after a few hours reminiscing they decided to head back home. Upon returning the two friends parted, the driver settling down in his flat, his friend retiring to the flat above. In the night the man in the bottom flat awoke to the sound of tapping on his window and in the darkness could make out the figure of a man at the window. Thinking it was his friend from upstairs he thought nothing of it, shouted at his friend and fell back to sleep. At around 3 a.m. the tapping started again, and the pet cat seemed spooked. This time the witness got to his feet and approached the back door only to find that the security light had not come on. Upon peering up to his neighbours flat he realised his neighbour was fast asleep as his apartment was in darkness. Stranger still, there was no way that anyone could get to the window to tap on it as there was a large and heavy garden table in the way. Rather unnerved by the episode the witness retired back to bed. The next day the man spoke to his neighbour about what had happened and was rather surprised to learn that he too had been woken by the same tapping noise. The following night the strange tapping noise started to plague the upstairs flat again and investigations proved fruitless, despite the fact the noises continued all week and then suddenly stopped. The witnesses believed that by visiting their former haunts they'd possibly brought back with them some type of apparition.

A haunted home

I'm indebted to a Chris Parsons for the following details. Chris lives with his wife Janet in Chelsfield at Bucks Cross Cottages which is situated close to Chelsfield Park Hospital. In January 2013 he contacted me with his story.

> Originally my house [No. 3] was built in the 1500s, although the cellar appears older. It was mentioned as a 'small school for poor children' in Cox's *Magna Brittanica*, from about 1720. The school ran the whole length of the attic and was reached by a wide staircase. The house has also been a gamekeeper's cottage and a small laundry serving Chelsfield House (now Chelsfield Park Hospital). The laundry was added in the late 1700s and about that time the house was divided into two dwellings with a new staircase being constructed to serve No. 4.
>
> There had been a few previous tenants. More importantly, there have also been several unusual occurrences. Keys that were left in the front door (inside) would swing for hours at a time. Doors would open and shut for no apparent reason. One windy night the door to the sitting-room rattled and rattled. Exasperated I said, 'Oh for God's sake come in then!' The door suddenly opened. I was very scared but there was no-one there. On another occasion two pictures

Bucks Cross Cottages in Chelsfield.

The haunted bathroom.

moved sideways after the death of a relative, the kitchen door suddenly opened wide without warning, and I said, 'Would you mind shutting the door, please?' and the door closed! Rings have reported been pulled from ladies' fingers never to be found, despite the room being close-carpeted and fully searched. People have been pushed into radiators when painting them. Enid Saunders who lived at No. 4 once reported 'creatures' scampering over her whilst in bed – it was not her cat. On another occasion when I was in bed I saw a large, dark-coloured figure at the end of the bed. Then there was the time that an early boyfriend of my daughter, Jane, who was supposedly psychic, went through all the rooms in the house. He declared that all rooms were 'clear' except the bathroom, where he said there 'was a weak male or a strong female presence.' It was in this room, previously a bedroom that in 1938 a thirteen-year-old boy named John had died from diphtheria. He is buried in St Martin's churchyard.

One of my daughter's female friends pooh-poohed the idea of ghosts and hauntings. Jane told her to go and 'Check in the bathroom, then' and after doing so the girl left the house, ashen-faced and visibly scared. On another occasion Enid told me that she had seen Maude, a former tenant, in the garden of No. 4, pegging out washing, this was in 1990. Maude had died in 1942! Other people who have lived in and visited the house have reported unusual feelings as if being closely examined by an unseen presence. This would make sense as some of the doors have observation panels in them, whilst other rooms have bolts on the outside of the room! Then there was the time in May 1994, about 1:30 a.m.,

I made a crude sign on a piece of box-wood entitled 'School Room', with black felt-tip pen and Tippex. On fixing the sign in the attic (School Room) the clock in the sitting room below struck three. The clock had not been wound for at least three months and showed the time as ten minutes to nine. On the same day a five-gallon carton of home-made beer stopped fermenting and would not be re-started. The weather was warm (May). A possible but ghostly reason for the clock striking three was provided by an Australian visitor. He suggested that three was the time that school was out. It still doesn't really explain why an unwound clock should suddenly burst into life.

In December 1995 friends of my wife, named Margery and Cedric visited the house for the first time. Margery, in the past, had dabbled in antiques and had acquired a crystal ball. She also had involved herself in séances as a medium. We mentioned a bit of the history of the place but Margery was sceptical. She was apprehensive about visiting the bathroom but nothing happened. I subsequently tapped on the wall to demonstrate how flimsy the construction was. An hour or so later, Margery asked, 'You know when you tapped on the wall?' Yes, I said. 'Did you hear the tapping coming back?' No, I said, there was no-one in the next room.

The most recent event was just after Christmas 2012 when I left the house via the kitchen door. The door was slammed shut with such force that plaster fell. It was not my wife who was in the sitting-room and there was no wind. Someone seemed unhappy! On a final note, we discovered an inglenook fireplace in 1996. It had Tudor tiles and was very similar in design to the fireplace in the Bo Peep pub … in the fireplace we also found some bones!

Doors with boarded-up observation panels and bolts on the outside suggest these rooms at Bucks Cross Cottages were once used to discipline children. Do the disciplinarians still haunt the building?

I was so intrigued by this reputedly haunted house, and the discovery of the mysterious bones that on a rainy Sunday in February 2013, accompanied by my wife Jemma, I visited the Parsons' household. After hearing of such weird activity I fully expected the house at Bucks Cross to have a sinister atmosphere, but how wrong could I have been. We were met not only by Chris and his wife, but a warm, welcoming atmosphere, made all the more cosy by a still smouldering open fire. The view from the house across the fields was beautiful, but inside the house there was even more atmosphere as Chris showed us several allegedly haunted locations including the bathroom where the teenager had died in the 1930s. The atmosphere was not at all unpleasant; every room seemed comforting, although my wife was rather spooked by the African guardian spirit doll that Chris has purchased many years

Chris and Janet Parsons standing in front of their fireplace. Chris is holding two of the mysterious bones.

ago from Papua New Guinea. We were extremely intrigued by many of the doors in the house which had bolts on the outside and patched up observation holes which suggested that many years ago people, possibly young children had been locked in some of the rooms.

Alongside the occasional bowed ceiling, tucked away hidey-holes, and old walls the most spectacular sight was the great Tudor fireplace which Chris unearthed several years ago. Chris showed us several photos from when he had discovered the hearth and spoke of finding several bottles and those strange bones which he fetched from a carrier bag. I was expecting to see the bones of a small mammal such as a cat, dog or fox, or even a bird but a majority of the bones clearly belonged to a much larger creature. I hoped that such bones were not from a human, although deep down had a feeling that the skeletal remains (which were mostly just a pile of leg bones) were of cattle. I had the photographs analysed by several people including a palaeontologist who was of the opinion that the larger bones were indeed from a cow and that the smaller remains were from a carnivore such as a dog or fox. I wondered why such bones had been placed in the fireplace, but considering the size of the hearth it seemed that the cow had possibly been roasted and eaten and the bones discarded. Another researcher believed the smaller bones were from a pig which would also make sense.

Another, albeit more far-fetched possibility, was that the animal bones had been placed in the fireplace to ward off evil spirits, although this act usually involved items of clothing such as shoes or smaller animals such as domestic cats. During the medieval period such items and other oddments may have been placed in a wall cavity as protection. Shoes were often used as spirit traps, and the remains of domestic cats – often associated with witches – were placed in the fireplace possibly to block off such a potential witch entrance. Cats were also perceived as being sensitive to spirits and their remains placed accordingly to ward off such spectral intruders. Mind you, another, more down to earth explanation is that the bones may have simply been piled within the wall to provide insulation.

A friend of mine named Emma told me, 'I remember at school learning that when building houses in the old days bones (legs) of cows were used around fireplaces to strengthen the wall above the fireplace without it burning or losing heat. As wooden beams were expensive they used rubble to insulate the walls too. There may be even more bones behind those walls. Also, old wives tales say bones of ritualistic animals above the fire increases fertility of the women of the house … as a gift to the spirits in return for a child.'

The latter fertility possibility doesn't sound so far-fetched and ties in once again with the placing of items. According to Ellen Leslie in *Country Life* from 10 January 2012 shoes were considered a symbol of fertility and also placed in walls and under floorboards.

I'll keep you up to date, however, should Mr and Mrs Parsons' start seeing the ghost of a cow in their house!

As we left Bucks Cross Cottages and braved the rain, Chris left us with a more recent incident involving a dinner party guest. Chris commented, 'Just twelve hours before you came one of the female guests was walking along the corridor that leads to the bathroom in the converted laundry when they stated quite matter-of-factly, upon returning to the dining area, that they'd sensed a presence in the hall.'

Just some of the odd bones found by Chris Parsons in the fireplace at Bucks Cross Cottages. The larger bones are thought to be of cattle, the smaller ones (only one appears here) a mixture of pig and fox or dog.

Whether it was the strongly observant spirit, or the unseen presence that likes to slam the doors we'll never know, and whilst the house, according to those who've experienced it, is haunted, the most unusual aspect of it all is the fact that Janet Parsons has never had a ghostly encounter in the house. She concluded, 'I feel very happy here, and if there is something here I would need to see it,' and with that I and my wife left Chris, Janet and the resident spooks to their own devices.

14

CHILLS AT CHISLEHURST

Chislehurst is a suburban settlement and home to more than 20,000 people. The area was once known as Ceosol Hyrst from Anglo Saxon. The first part of the name possibly derives from Chesil or Chisel, meaning stony or gravelled, and hurst suggests woodland. Chislehurst Caves, situated at Old Hill was the setting in 1972 for the filming of the six-part *Doctor Who* episode 'The Mutants'. The 1982 horror film *Inseminoid* and popular BBC series *Merlin* was also filmed there. On a dark night in 1863 a meteor 'the size of the moon' was reported as passing over Chislehurst Common. A witness to the phenomenon wrote to *The Times* that, '…it so illumined the inside of the carriage that I could easily have read *The Times…*'

A few chills

The Queens Head public house at Chislehurst sits at No. 2 in the High Street and to be honest it doesn't exactly look like how you'd imagine a haunted inn should look. The modern furnishings and its location, next to a pond and in a busy High Street shouldn't put you off however. The ghostly activity here is, like so many pubs before it, vague and sporadic. The spectre manifests itself to both customers and staff who usually report glasses flying off the bar. Those who believe it to be the work of a pesky apparition blame a former reveller who used to frequent the pub many years ago. The drinker was so regular in fact, that he expected every pint he consumed to be put on his tab. The landlord at the time was happy to go along with this but when the pub was closed down and taken over by new owners, the succeeding landlord was not happy for customers to have a tab. This, of course, upset the regular who one day marched into the pub demanding a drink but was turned away due to his aggressive behaviour. Legend has it that the next day the heavy drinker was found dead; face down in the nearby pond. It seems that due to being of poor health, and of little money, he'd committed suicide by drowning himself in the waterhole.

The Queens Head at Chislehurst is the haunt of a former customer.

The pond next to the Queens Head pub. The waterhole was said to have claimed the life of a man who now reputedly haunts the pub.

The Bickley restaurant and bar at Chislehurst.

Another haunted public house in Chislehurst is the Bickley, a gastro pub situated on the Chislehurst Road in close proximity to the caves. The building dates back to 1870. On 24 February 1983 the *Bromley Times* spoke of the 'white lady' said to haunt the pub. The ghost was said to haunt room No. 2. According to the newspaper, the ghost 'is rumoured to be the same one that haunts nearby Chislehurst caves' and often leaves cold spots in areas of the building she has loitered. At the time the landlady, Mary Cross, commented, 'My sister Renee was frightened when she was in the room one day and she saw a shadow at the door. She thought it was one of the children larking around but it wasn't.'

Scadbury Manor is a medieval moated manor house which sits in Scadbury Park, which is 300 acres of glorious woodland. The building has connections to the Walsingham family who from 1424 settled in the area, and stayed for two centuries. The original settlers in the area were the de Scathbury's who may have taken their name from the place which is first mentioned in the thirteenth century. The name of 'Scadbury' is of Anglo-Saxon origins and means 'shady hill'. Today, the house, which is a set of eerie-looking remains, is open to the public and can be accessed by a series of woodland paths. Writing for *Wiki Kent*, researcher Wendy Stevenson describes the setting as 'haunting' and 'evocative' and so it doesn't seem that unusual that ghosts are occasionally reported there. Some say that the Walsingham's still linger in the place they settled in all those centuries ago. The sound of horses hooves on cobbles has been reported on some of the pathways, an eerie cacophony indeed should one be strolling through the grounds at dusk or on a misty morning. Many may ask why there should be the

sound of cobbles when the ruins are set in woodland, but recent excavations have unearthed a cobbled pathway that lead up to the house.

Due to the history of the area it's no wonder that avid ghost hunters have taken to the park in search of rumoured spooks. Several groups have looked into the alleged hauntings of the area but it appears that the activity is inconsistent. Investigative results have varied depending on the researchers present. Some have reported strange smells such as rotting meat and burning, bringing some people to conclude that this may have been the spiritual remnants of the fire that destroyed the property many years ago. Other researchers reported the sounds of hissing and also footsteps, but again, with the reports being so vague one is inclined to believe that a majority of the alleged paranormal occurrences are more likely connected to the psyche of an individual rather than a certain place. One research group who visited the ruins claimed to have photographed a strange, swirling mist, but upon analysis the photograph appears to show the breath of the person taking the photograph. Again, it's fair to say that the mind runs wild with such an environment, and ghost-hunters are all too keen to take photographs in the hope they may find an unusual – although not paranormal – orb in their picture. The fact that there are no recorded ghost stories from the manor could well suggest that the building is simply atmospheric, but nothing more.

The creepy caves

In early April 2009 it was rumoured that pop superstar Michael Jackson, who passed away in the June of the same year,

Chislehurst Caves can be found on Old Hill not far from Chislehurst Railway Station.

was going to rent (Foxbury Manor) a property in Chislehurst before embarking on a fifty-date concert tour of London. Although the singer died before the concerts began, several major tabloids at the time of the rumour claimed that the house, which was said to have cost £1 million to rent, was situated near the haunted caves of Chislehurst. Whether 'Jacko' really was going to move to Kent we'll never know, maybe the publicity was nothing more than an April Fool's prank but the paranormal activity within the caves was of no doubt. According to the *Telegraph* of 28 March 2009, 'Ghost sightings have been reported at the caves, which were dug in the chalk by Saxons, Druids and Romans.'

Who knows whether Jackson was aware of the reputed ghostly activity, but each year the caves do attract a number of tourists and ghost-hunters intrigued

by the spook tales said to originate from within the twenty or so mile stretch of tunnels. Despite being called caves, the subterranean network of tunnels are actually man-made rather than of natural formation. They were carved through a chalk hill a few hundred feet below ground over the course of a few thousand years; although a majority, according to historian John Vigar were dug out in the eighteenth and nineteenth century. In his booklet *Chislehurst Caves: A Short History*, historian Dr Eric Inman states, 'In August 1903 William Nichols, a local resident and Vice-President of the British Archaeological Association startled that organisation by pronouncing a theory that the three Chislehurst mines were made by the Romans, Saxons and Druids respectively, the names by which they are known to this day. His ideas are presumably based on stories current locally at the time reinforced by the layout and direction of the chambers ...'

Writing in his book *The Ghosts of Chislehurst Caves*, researcher James Wilkinson states that, 'There is no direct evidence in the surrounding areas of the caves to say that Druids were here,' but, 'Evidence of the Roman occupation of Britain can be found in Chislehurst.'

During the 1930s the caves were used as a mushroom factory, but the onset of the Second World War put pay to any potential tourism. Thousands of adults and children inhabited the ill-lit passageways for shelter from the bombs; children would find the labyrinthine network a great place for fun and adventure, completely unaware of the bombs that were falling high above them. In the 1950s the caves became an ideal venue for jazz concerts, and this would flourish into the 1960s and '70s when

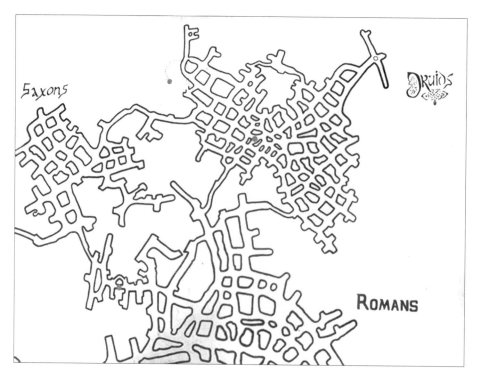

The map at the caves entrance shows the vast network of tunnels.

famous musicians such as Jimi Hendrix, Cream, David Bowie, The Yardbirds, Pink Floyd, and The Animals, played there. Members of Led Zeppelin were said to have thrown a party in the caves in 1974 whilst concerts continued sporadically into the 1990s. Nowadays the caves are open to the public, accessible via their Old Hill location. Guided tours take place on the hour.

Over the years numerous ghost stories have emerged from those pitch black passageways and if ever proven true, they could well make the caves one of the most haunted locations on the planet. Sadly, none of these ghost stories can be proven scientifically, unless of course such entities are filmed or photographed in all of their ghoulish glory and so until that time, we must accustom ourselves with the foggy legends.

The cavalier

In January of 2013 I visited the caves. It was a mild morning when I strolled into the entrance, visited the gift shop and was taken into the mines by guide Jason Desporte. In the darkness, only armed with a flickering oil lamp, we trudged through the passageways for almost an hour. I was thrilled by the atmosphere as the lantern light created eerie shadows on the wall. We explored a number of reputedly haunted spots but it wasn't until after we'd finished and traipsed back into the welcoming light that Jason spoke of the alleged cavalier spirit.

In the seventeenth century the Roundheads and the Cavaliers were involved in the Civil War. Rumour has it that one such cavalier lived in

During the Second World War thousands of people sought refuge in the caves. Just a few decades' later well-known rock bands played gigs in the ill-lit tunnels.

a house at nearby Old Hill. His plan was, should he ever be pursued by the enemy then he would escape via a passageway from his garden, leading him to the gloomy tunnels. The cavalier was said to have concealed an entrance/ trap to a shaft with leaves, and should the Roundheads approach this area by lantern light, they would no doubt plummet down the shaft. However, those who claim to have seen the ghost state that it is not one of these Roundheads haunting the area but a cavalier. Had he fallen down his own trap? According to James Wilkinson a ghostly cavalier has been seen in a section of tunnel by a former manager named Derek Hopkins. Others who've experienced the ghost claim to have heard its footsteps.

The Roman

A spectre of a Roman soldier was said to have been sighted by several children during the Second World War. They were playing in an area adjacent to a sectioned off area when the figure, in full garb, appeared. Sadly, sightings of the wraith seem extremely rare but it was believed that thousands of years ago the soldier was murdered outside the caves. Others claim that he was killed whilst setting up camp nearby to a stream.

Horses

In 1999 the now defunct television show *The Why Files* visited the caves. Tour guide Terry Hunt was interviewed by presenter Dave Barrett about the alleged hauntings.

Tour guide Jason Desporte leads a group into the darkness.

… like a doorway into the very bowels of Hell!

He stated that he was sceptical in view of the spook tales. A local author and historian named Dr Eric Inman when interviewed for the show remained convinced that Chislehurst Caves were haunted. He said, 'In the early 1980s the psychic research society [Society for Psychical Research] came down here and recorded some noises, such as whinnying horses.'

The spectral horse could be connected to a terrible accident that took place many years ago in the caves. There was once believed to have been a stable in the tunnels and it was said to have collapsed, killing one of its inhabitants.

The imp

A mischievous imp is said to haunt the tunnels. Tour guide Jason Desporte told me that when the caves were used as a mushroom factory, some of the workers would report the appearance of a small figure, something akin to a goblin that would try to prevent them working. Interestingly, in 2008 when the *Most Haunted* investigative team filmed in the caves, they too claimed to have picked up the presence of a similar malevolent boggart. Other researchers like to call the pesky spectre a hunchback, due to its huddled form. The humanoid is said to be of devilish origin, and have cloven hooves, but sightings of the imp have been all too vague to substantiate the legend.

The black dog and the black cat

When I visited the caves in January 2013 I asked Jason Desporte about an intriguing sketch that hung in the gift shop.

The image, showing a ferocious black wolf-like creature was given the title, 'Chislehurst Caves – Have you heard the call?' Jason stated that the illustration had been done by a former owner of the caves, and was in relation to a phantasmal black dog said to roam the mines. The hellhound was said to have burning red eyes as big as saucers but sightings were scant. Even so, Jason was quick to tell me, 'A few years ago I was in the tunnels and saw a fleeting shape, about 2ft in height that rushed down one of the passageways.' Belief is that the black dog is some type of Celtic manifestation conjured up to ward off evil spirits. Mind you, there is also the possibility that the ghost dog is far less malevolent and could well be the spirit of a dog once used for Edwardian tours of the caves. In James Wilkinson's book, he mentions two reports from guides Tony Roud and Dave Duker in regards to a large black animal seen about the caves. Rumour has it that the creature is a large black cat, something akin to a 'panther,' which would be the melanistic (dark pigment) form of the leopard. It has also been said that over the last twenty or so years there have been numerous reports from the wooded areas of Chislehurst concerning a similarly large cat. Even so, such a beast, if real – which I believe it is - would need to feed and the fact that the caves do not even harbour any rats, means that such an animal would find little in the tunnels to eat. Could the rumours of a ghostly creature be true?

The Druid

One of the most impressive areas of the caves is said to be that which harbours a Druid altar. There are said to be nine altars within the passageways, eight of these being rather small and rumoured to have once been used for animal sacrifice. The largest of the altars however has a more sinister history. This particular altar, which resembles a large chalk ledge or shelf, was rumoured to have once been used for human sacrifice! It's only natural that this section of the caves is creepy. It is the one area which seems to echo the most. It is also pitch black and said to be haunted by a cloaked figure. If you visit the gift shop of the caves you may be lucky enough to pick up a black and white postcard depicting the alleged ghost of a Druid. The photo was said to have been taken before the First World War and shows a transparent hooded figure standing in front of the largest altar. It's difficult to imagine a time when these individuals would have gathered in the tunnels to perform the occasional ritual sacrifice. James Wilkinson is quick to add that, 'In reality, this is all very unlikely to have happened in the Caves,' but it does add to the mystery of the place. There is also rumour of a ghostly Druid princess said to have perished in an underground stream. Sightings of the phantom female ceased after the Second World War.

The lady of the pool

One of the creepiest locations within the belly of the caves is the reputedly haunted pool. The waterhole can still be seen today but is only a couple of feet deep. It is around this section of the caves that the most paranormal activity is said to take place. More than two centuries previous a woman was said to have been murdered at this spot by her husband. Her body was thrown into the pool – it was much deeper back then – and weighed down with stones. There seems to be little evidence to prove this murder took place although according to Brian Williamson who edited the *Ghosts! – Creepy Tales from Chislehurst Caves* book, the local *Newsshopper* newspaper names the woman as one Mary Jane Beckett. It is said that ever since this alleged murder a ghostly woman dressed in white has been seen near the pool. On some occasions the spectre is seen, in forlorn state, perched on one of the rocks at the back of the pool. Stranger still, in the early 1940s excavations were said to have unearthed the skeletal remains of a human. Since then the ghostly sightings increased.

One of the more recent encounters with the ghost by the pool took place in 1957. Back then a reward of £5 was put forward by the owners of the cave to anyone brave enough to spend the night in the darkness. A policeman named Tony Bayfield accepted the challenge and sat by the pool. To bide his time in the blackness, and possibly to take his mind off the possible resident ghosts, he carved the figure of a horse into one of the chalk walls. It can still be seen today. However, the following day when

The alleged Druid altar said to have once been used for human sacrifice!

asked about his nightly vigil he mentioned seeing 'something' by the pool but never stated exactly what. Had Tony seen the loitering female ghost, or had his mind simply played ghoulish tricks in the darkness?

Children

From the war there are no reports of children who inhabited the mines having died in the caves. Although on a more cheerful note, a little girl was born in the hospital that was situated in one of the passageways. Rose Razzell was born one night in 1941. At the time pregnant women were usually transferred to a nearby hospital but due to the frequent raids upon the area, Rose's mother, Polly delivered her baby daughter there and then in those dimly lit mines. According to the *Newsshopper* of 6 October 2011, 'When Polly could not think of a middle name, the midwife who helped deliver Rose suggested Cavena as a reminder of the place she was born.'

The ghosts of giggling children have been heard on numerous occasions in the caves. Jason Desporte is one of the people said to have heard the eerie laughing. One

The haunted pool – a woman was said to have been murdered here centuries ago.

morning whilst doing a routine check of the caves, Jason was in the vicinity of the Roman well when he heard a noise behind him. It was the giggle of a little girl. Jason knew that there was no one else in the cave system and a shine of his torch revealed nothing. However, a short while after Jason heard the same giggling, this time further off into the distance. According to Jason a young girl had died whilst digging a hole above the entrance of the caves. She'd been with her brother at the time, during the war, but the chalk collapsed and killed her. Her brother survived. In some instances witnesses have reported the feeling of a small hand in their own whilst walking about the mines.

The tunnels today are empty except for a few life-sized models dotted about the place. One such figure is that of a little girl sitting on a bed in the hospital area. Jason told me, 'I like to call her *The Exorcist* girl because she looks a bit like the girl out of the horror film.' I didn't find the young girl particularly creepy but several tourists, particularly children, have been spooked by the mannequin. I'm pretty sure that if one was left alone in the tunnels of a night, the figures would prove to be an eerie presence. One figure that does tend to send the shivers down the spine is known as 'Gordon' and resembles a green-faced goblin. The model can be seen in a gloomy corridor and for added atmosphere is clutching a couple of model rats which he has just feasted on!

The Roman well

Who is the ghostly figure said to have been seen leaning over the well and peering down into the darkness? Is the

In the 1950s a police officer claimed a £5 reward by accepting the Chislehurst 'challenge' and stayed the night in the caves. In this photo Jason Desporte points out a carving of a horse on the wall which the man etched to pass the time.

Despite the bombing raids over Kent, no one who stayed in the caves during the Blitz was killed. However, a little girl was born there in 1941.

wraith also responsible for the unusual smells sometimes picked up by the well? Nobody seems to know.

The pram pusher

No one seems to know the story behind the sporadic reports of a ghostly young woman seen pushing a pram through the tunnels. Maybe in life the woman had died elsewhere, possibly due to a bombing raid, but why she has returned to the caves no one knows.

The whistler

The whistling ghost is another relatively vague spook said to be the spirit of a former guide named Derek. When the *Most Haunted* investigative team conducted a vigil they claimed to have heard somebody whistling.

More legends

Over the years parts of the tunnels have been used for Role Playing Games – groups dressed in medieval and fantasy attire acting out scenes of chivalry. Nowadays due to health and safety regulations general visitors are only allowed into the tunnels for a guided tour, which is understandable considering how dark and complex the network of caves is. The last £5 challenge was offered a few decades now. According to the *Bromley Times* of 26 October 2012, on the Halloween of 1985 two guides, David Duker and Chris Perry, accepted the £5 challenge. They were to settle down in the caves for a twelve-hour vigil,

Is that the ghoulish imp said to wander the tunnels? No, it's merely 'Gordon', a life-size model mocked up by the staff.

armed only with a tape recorder so as to avoid any tomfoolery. According to researcher James Wilkinson the challenge actually took place on 2 November, because the Halloween had fallen on the Thursday making it more difficult for the men to spend the night in the caves due to other commitments. They both carved

Chislehurst Caves are said to harbour at least ten spirits.

In 2010 a ghost hunt was conducted in the caves.

This way for spooks!

a plaque into the wall before nestling into their sleeping bags at separate passageways. At approximately 2:30 a.m. Dave was awoken by the cries and groans of his friend Chris. Dave rushed to his friends' aid only to realise that there was a major problem with Chris. Dave, realising they had locked themselves in, searched for the keys in vain but eventually sought help from a rescue team stationed outside the main door. Eventually Chris was lifted from the caves and taken to Queen Mary's Hospital in Sidcup where he was checked over. All seemed to be fine until a bruise began to develop on his shoulder and an x-ray revealed a dislocation. According to Brian Williamson's book, 'The doctors said that it looked as though someone (or something?) had pulled his arm violently upwards, as though trying to drag him away.'

In James Wilkinson's book it is stated that Chris suffered a personality change after that night in the caves, and can't actually remember the vigil. Some say he suffered some type of fit, but whatever the case, the curse of the Chislehurst challenge was mentioned in some of the major tabloids at the time.

On another occasion during the late 1940s, when the caves were in disuse it is claimed that a religious fanatic broke into the tunnels and after becoming lost was found dead the following week; the verdict being that he'd died of fright. His body, which was discovered by some youths, was naked and his torch switched off. His fingernails were said to have been worn down suggesting he'd spent his last hours clambering around the walls trying to find a way out. According to Brian Williamson the body was of twenty-six-year-old John Richardson. He adds that the man '… told his family that he was going on a walking holiday, but he apparently found his way into the caves where he fasted naked in darkness, presumably while meditating.' It's possible the man may have perished due to exhaustion and hunger.

Many of these legends tend to vary over the years depending on the story-teller, and this inconsistency to some extent keeps these legends alive. For instance, there are some who will say that those who've ventured into the tunnels of a night have perished at the hands of the 'lady of the lake,' the forlorn spectre who was murdered all those years ago. Others claim to have seen strange ghostly green lights, others will speak of eerie mists, peculiar cold spots, fleeting shadows, and feeling unseen hands tugging on garments. Add this to the already growing number of legends pertaining to people who've claimed to have seen phantom figures of men and women, and you have a whole host of ghosts.

In 2010 *Newshopper* reporter Vicki Foster, accompanied by two friends, Yana Barrett and Stevie Masters, visited the caves under the cloak of darkness in the hope of shedding further light on some of these classic, albeit debatable, yarns. She was part of an investigation conducted by *London Paranormal*. This had been her first ever ghost-hunt. She reported, 'I did not know what to expect. Beforehand we were told some scary tales of events at the caves, including one about a man who had his arm ripped off while sleeping there during an all-night challenge.'

A medium had been present at the time of the vigil and claimed to have contacted the spirit of a young girl called Megan. Perhaps by complete coincidence, Yana claimed that straight afterwards someone or some 'thing' had pulled her

Plaque on wall outside the caves.

hair and their nostrils were filled with a sweet odour. The groups experienced the sound of a few dull thuds and at one point claimed to have heard a distinctive growl suggesting some large animal form was present – were they in the company of the shaggy dog-like creature? Other members of the group claimed to experience unusual things, with several participants reporting on weird tapping noises, and also sudden pains which dissipated when the group moved between different areas. These types of experiences seem relatively common in ghost investigations. Sceptics argue that when a number of people get together for such a vigil that senses are heightened and the minds of the participants begin to play tricks.

Whatever your theories regarding the spooks of Chislehurst caves, there can be no doubt as to the dank atmosphere of the place. However, for a place rarely even frequented by spiders and bats, there seems no real reason for ghosts and ghouls to be present. Nevertheless the next time you're standing in those dark tunnels with your lantern flickering way, always be sure to look behind you.

15

ENCOUNTER AT ELMSTEAD

The residential district of Elmstead can be found between Mottingham, Bickley, Bromley and Chislehurst. It is often known as Elmstead Woods after the ancient woodland which can be found there.

Someone at the top of the stairs

One story which springs to mind regarding ghostly encounters in Elmstead comes from a woman who a few years ago had started to rent a house from a vicar in the neighbourhood. One afternoon the woman was upstairs in her bedroom unpacking a bag when she saw the figure of an elderly man at the top of the stairs. Suddenly, the frightened witness heard a male voice in her head which said, 'This is how I died' and with that the ghostly figure tumbled down the staircase.

The woman was so terrified that she raced out of the house – not once looking for the male figure – and sought the nearest pub for a drink to calm her nerves. When she eventually returned to the house there was no sign of the man.

16

MOTTINGHAM MYSTERY

Although Mottingham is a district of south London it is located 'at the convergence of the London Borough of Bromley, the London Borough of Lewisham and the Royal Borough of Greenwich.' In AD 862 Mottingham was recorded as Modingahema. Historian John Marius Wilson described Mottingham in the nineteenth century as 'a hamlet in Eltham parish.' On 4 August 1585 a rather unusual event occurred in Mottingham. A field belonging to a Sir Percival Hart suddenly sank, revealing a large hole that swallowed several trees. A record from the time states that 'the compass of the hole was about 80 yards' with a depth so vast that no one could 'find or feel any bottom.'

Shadowy figure ...

In 2009 a subscriber to the website for This Is Local London spoke of living in a haunted house and the fear of ridicule after reporting such an encounter. The person, who remained anonymous, stated that she'd spent many years previously in a haunted house and believed the spectre followed the family wherever they went. When she moved to Mottingham in the 1990s she claimed to have seen the shadowy figure of a child which drifted down the stairs. The witness added, 'It was a bit scary, but whatever it was must have followed me from house to house.' Despite this experience unnerving her she concluded, 'I don't want it to go as it hasn't done me any harm.'

A vast majority of alleged ghost encounters tend to be very vague, but if we add up all of these fleeting experiences then it would suggest that a lot of people are having extraordinary sightings that cannot all be explained.

17

ANOMALY AT ANERLEY

The district of Anerley was once recorded as Annerley and regarded as a village on the Croydon railway. It is, like every other place in this book, part of the London borough of Bromley, and it was once the site of the Crystal Palace, an iron and plate-glass building used for exhibitions. Walter de la Mare, a writer of ghost stories, used to reside in Anerley at Thornsett Road.

Care home scare!

Paul Masters, mentioned in the West Wickham segment spoke of a possible haunted care home in Anerley. According to Paul:

> A woman used to work in a care home looking after disabled children and many of the staff had reported footsteps and dragging noises from the office/store room upstairs while they were working. Every time they would go and investigate the noises they would find nothing except the occasional object that had been moved. Many of the staff did not want to be alone at night in the building. One night these workers had a new child stay and during the night one worker thought she saw the child walking at the end of the hall. She called out to him but he didn't respond and turned the corner. The care worker thought that the child must have needed to use the toilet and so she hurried to his aid only to find no trace of the child. As you can imagine, the worker was very confused as there was no other way back past her. She went to the new boys' bed room only to find him fast asleep. Naturally, she refused to work nights alone after that.

Anerley Hill horror

A stretch of Anerley Hill, which runs from Crystal Palace toward Anerley Road, was once rumoured to be haunted. An old cottage that used to stand on the hill was reputedly so ghost-infested that the owner was very keen to sell the property. One evening when the owner was sitting in her front room watching television one of the doors slammed shut. The witness was also plagued by phantom footsteps during the night. They would approach the door of the living room and then suddenly turn and ascend the stairs.

Nearby Crystal Palace has a haunted history, but not all the ghostly tales come under the Bromley borough. However, there is a creepy legend concerning an old train which is said to be buried in a disused tunnel beneath Crystal Palace Park. In the past local children would tell the story of how all those on board still remain, embedded in the soil, and that on occasion their hands attempt to claw to the surface. Maybe this lost train was the last of its kind to travel on the Crystal Palace pneumatic railway which only ran for a year from 1864 to 1865. Remnants of a tunnel were said to have been unearthed in 1992, whilst legend of its eerie inhabitants may have stemmed from 1978 when a woman claimed to have found the secret tunnel, and encased within it a mouldy carriage complete with skeletons dressed in tatty Victorian attire. This story has become an urban legend over the years. Author John Brooks however has found several holes in the rumour stating, '… though there were accounts of a ghost train complete with skeleton passengers being discovered when a girl fell down a shaft in 1978, the buried train is really an experimental one that was driven by compressed air.'

This project was made redundant after a year and the train simply bricked up. There were no passengers.

In 2009 historians visited the hidden basement of a Crystal Palace pub called the White Hart. Several secret rooms, hidden from public view for many years, were unearthed. A secret tunnel was also found leading some locals to believe that smugglers had once operated in the area. There were also legends that the dusty basement was haunted by the spirit of a little girl. And speaking of subterranean horrors, a tunnel, said to run between Gipsy Hill and the Crystal Palace stations, has long been rumoured to be the haunt of a track-maintenance worker. The ghost, sometimes described as headless, is attributed to the tale of a worker who was decapitated, many years ago, in the tunnel when an approaching train ran him down.

One of the weirdest legends to originate from Crystal Palace is mentioned in Eric Maple's book *The Realm of Ghosts*. In it he speaks of a peculiar apparition that appeared over London in 1832, he states, 'the outbreak of the cholera epidemic was accompanied by the vision of a flaming sword seen by thousands in the sky … This was a sign. A century later, when the last symbol of the Victorian Age – the Crystal Palace – caught fire, old men and women looked out of their windows at the red light in the sky and murmured, 'It is a sign' – a sign that the old ways and the old world were doomed.

18

THE PETT'S WOOD GHOST

The area of Petts Wood possibly gets its name from the fact that before becoming a suburb it was a wood. 'Pett' originated from the Pett family who were leaders in the field of shipbuilding.

Terrified Tom

One of the only ghost stories I could find connected to Petts Wood concerned a man named Tom. Many years ago Tom would walk to and from work via Chislehurst Common, taking in woodland along the way. Tom always walked home alone, frequenting those remote spots where centuries previous highwaymen had prowled. It was a December night, there had just been a heavy snowfall, and the tranquillity of the night was only interrupted by the crunch of the pristine white beneath Tom's weary feet. Every now and then he would flash his torch across the pathway, but at a certain spot Tom was alerted to a dull thudding sound that grew louder and louder. Suddenly there was an icy grip upon his already cold neck, Tom spun around, lashing out aggressively only to find nothing except a rustle in some nearby foliage. Tom, his senses heightened could feel his body consumed by a suffocating terror and then, seconds later the apparition appeared. It was the figure of a man – darkly clad – upon a great and equally dark horse. Its hooves thudded on the white ground, causing snow to fall from a branch and onto Tom's head and shoulders. In terror he flapped at the snow, and stood, with his torch beam cast across the ground where he could make out a set of impressions as if made by a galloping horse. There was no sign of the horse and rider and so, rather bravely, Tom decided to follow the phantom prints. Tom trudged on, now aware of a further snowfall, when suddenly he was conscious of a choking smoke and flashing lights around him. Tom ran from the scene and in sheer terror scrambled to his doorstep and into the arms of his wife.

Within minutes Tom's wife had poured him a whiskey to warm his cockles, and it was then that he relayed his bizarre experience. The *Petts Wood & District Advertiser* who mentioned the story in 1946 asked whether Tom had not actually seen nothing more than a passing train after getting lost in the darkness. However could a man who spent night after night walking home through the woods have been mistaken? Well, I leave you with the last words of the *Advertiser* who conclude that '...the day was Christmas Eve, and before reaching the path in the woods, Tom's route had taken him by at least three of Chislehurst's most popular hostelries!' Had Tom become disorientated due to too much drink, or had he experienced ghostly phenomena?

19

GHOULS OF GREEN STREET GREEN

The unusual name of Green Street Green is said to originate from 'la grenestrete' meaning 'green' or 'grassy' hamlet. In 1862 the *Bromley Record* mentions the discovery of a mammoth tooth found in a gravel pit. In 1922 a mammoth tusk was also unearthed.

The Queens Head

On 30 March 2001 the *Orpington Times* spoke of the intriguing history of the Queens Head public house, and its ghost. The spectre, according to then manager Lorraine Wormsley, was one which liked to traipse up and down one of the corridors. She reported to the newspaper, 'Footsteps have been heard running up and down the corridor but when staff have gone to look there's been no one there.'

In addition to this traipsing spectre there is a legend that the last highwayman in England was hanged from a

The Queens Head at Green Street Green.

gallows that used to sit outside the pub. Maybe it's his fleeting phantom sometimes recorded as being seen outside the inn. The Queens Head can be found at No. 73 in the High Street.

'And all those people who scoff, well, they are not just sceptical – they are downright afraid.'
Peggy Martyn Clark, Secretary of Kentish Authors Group (1964)

BIBLIOGRAPHY

Books

Arnold, Neil, *Mystery Animals of the British Isles: Kent* (CFZ Press, 2009)

Arnold, Neil, *Mystery Animals of the British Isles: London* (CFC Press, 2011)

Arnold, Neil, *Paranormal London* (The History Press, 2010)

Bennett, Ernest, *Apparitions & Haunted Houses* (David & Charles, 2012)

Borrowman, Robert, *Beckenham Past & Present* (T.W. Thornton, 1910)

Brooks, John, *The Good Ghost Guide* (Jarrold, 1994)

Cassirer, Manfred, *The Bromley Poltergeist* (Privately Published, 1993)

Dunkin, John, *Outlines of the History and Antiquities of Bromley, in Kent* (Self-published, 1815)

Fort, Charles, *Wild Talents* (John Brown Publishing, 1998)

Green, Andrewm *Our Haunted Kingdom* (Fontana, 1974)

Green, Andrew, *Haunted Kent Today* (SB Publications, 1999)

Hippisley Cox, Anthony D., *Haunted Britain* (Pan McMillan, 1973)

Horsburgh, E.L.S., *Bromley* (Hodder & Stoughton, 1929)

Howell, George (ed.), *The Kentish Notebook* (Smither Brothers, 1891)

Inman, Dr Eric, *Chislehurst Caves, A Short History* (Kent Mushrooms Ltd, 1996)

Jerrold, Walter, *Highways & Byways of Kent* (Macmillan & Co., 1907)

Long, Roger, *Haunted Inns of Kent* (SB Publications, 2005)

Lysons, Daniel, *The Environs of London: Volume 4: Counties of Herts, Essex and Kent* (McMillan, 1796)

Maple, Eric, *The Realm of Ghosts* (Pan, 1964)

Ogley, Bob, *The Ghosts of Biggin Hill* (Froglets, 2001)

Spencer, John and Anne, *The Encyclopaedia of Ghosts & Spirits* (Headline, 2001)

Stead, William Thomas, *Real Ghost Stories* (1891)

Underwood, Peter, *Ghosts of Kent* (Meresborough Books, 1985)

Wilkinson, James, *The Ghosts of Chislehurst Caves* (Paintpop Limited, 2011)

Williamson, Brian (ed.), *Ghosts! Creepy Tales from Chislehurst Caves* (Null Publishing, 2012)

Other

The Bromley Record & Monthly Advertiser
   (Edward Strong Printers, Market Square 1865)

Websites

www.ancientmonuments.info
www.banstedhistory.com
www.beastsoflondon.blogspot.com
www.bromley.gov.uk
www.bromleytimes.co.uk
www.chislehurst.co.uk
www.chislehurst-caves.co.uk
www.edithsstreets.blogspot.co.uk
www.ghostconnections.com

www.ghosts-uk.net
www.guardian.co.uk
www.kentmonsters.blogspot.com
www.londonnet.co.uk
www.newsshopper.co.uk
www.paranormaldatabase.com
www.roadghosts.com
www.sundridgepark.com
www.thebopeep.com
www.thebullsheadpub.net
www.thecrowninnleavesgreen.co.uk
www.thisiskent.co.uk
www.thisislocallondon.co.uk
www.wikikent.co.uk
www.yourcounty.co.uk